## A Foster S...

'The King's face ... ... when he
heard the news. Then he cursed so loud and long
that monks flew in all directions like scalded
cats. The monastery bell tolled out, then the
cathedral bell, then the bell of St. Peter's. Soon
every fighting man was running in alarm to
Ferns. MacMurrough ripped off his monk's
robes. Then he buckled on his great sword and
bounded out through the gates, white with fright
and fury.

He had not taken four strides outside the
abbey gates when he was recognized.

'The King! The King!' the cry went up.
'MacMurrough is back!' The news spread like
wildfire and before long the old battlecry rose
across the crowds, 'MacMurrough Aboo!...'

And so the stage is set for one of the most
dramatic events in Irish history – the Norman
Invasion.

*Nicholas Furlong*

# A Foster Son for a King

*Illustrated by Terry Myler*

HAWTHORN BOOKS

*The Children's Press*

*In happy memory of*
**Brendan Hearne**
*2B, S.P.C. and 1943.*

First published in 1986 by
The Children's Press
90 Lower Baggot Street, Dublin 2

© Text Nicholas Furlong
© Illustrations The Children's Press

This book is published with the financial
assistance of the Arts Council
(An Chomhairle Ealaion), Dublin

ISBN 0 947962 03 4 paperboards
ISBN 0 947962 04 2 paper

Typesetting by Computertype Ltd.
Printed in Ireland by Mount Salus Press.

# Contents

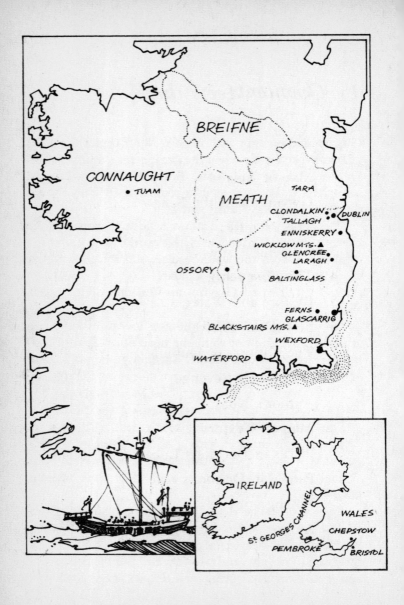

# 1 Gwynn Meets the King

Gwynn was playing with his dog Wuff under the walls of Pembroke Castle when the great gates slammed shut. He jumped up in alarm. Even Wuff growled and scratched at the gates as if to remind them they should not have been shut until sunset.

The reason for the dramatic closing soon became clear. A band of intruders with swords came marching up the hill from the water's edge, and a rough untidy crowd of cutthroats they looked.

'Pirates!' gasped Gwynn, as Wuff set off to attack them.

He whistled and called the dog in vain, then raced after him. He did not want the head of his faithful rat-hunter and watchdog cut off. But though he ran as hard as he could, when he caught up with the marching men Wuff was already at war. Every hair on his body abristle, he was jumping up and down, barking ferociously.

The band of roughs had come to a halt. A huge man, savage in appearance, with a square head of greying curls and a beard, pushed forward and addressed Wuff.

'God bless and save us,' he said. 'We are to be eaten alive!'

Then the savage man clapped his eyes on Gwynn, who looked up into the big man's face, terrified. It was a rough weather-beaten face, with a battle scar from the forehead to the jaw, and two very bright blue eyes which shone as clear as a spring well. He was their leader for sure, because as he frowned at Gwynn one of his men said:

'Will we eat him, MacMurrough?'

The big man reached down and plucked Gwynn right up into his arms. Gwynn waited for him to open his mouth, for he was certain now that he was a cannibal. Then the big face creased into a smile as sudden as a sunburst.

'Certainly not!' he shouted. 'We will ask him questions instead.'

Putting Gwynn down on the ground he went on, 'You look very important to me. I'll bet you're a spy in the pay of the Earl of Pembroke. That's what you are, I swear ... a spy!'

Gwynn would have liked to be taken for a spy but he thought better of pretending that he was, for the men before him looked very wicked.

'No, I am not,' he said. 'But I know all about the Earl ... and everyone in Pembroke.'

The big man's eyes opened wide.

'You know *all* about *everyone* in Pembroke! Did you hear that, men? You must be very clever to know all that. Bless my soul, none of my men know half what you know. I'm beginning to like you. I think I really must appoint you as one of my guides. You see ... it's a long time since I've been here. Yes, I played here, on this very ground, with a boy like you and a dog ... oh, well ... it must be hundreds of years ago....' Then there was an abrupt change of mood.

'Does a man called Strongbow live here?' The big man looked down into Gwynn's face, watching every twitch of his muscles through half-closed eyes.

'He used to live in this very castle,' said Gwynn,

pointing to the great stone fortress, 'and he had hundreds of men and lots of gold, but then he gave trouble to the king and the king came and threw him out, and now he goes around Wales like a beggar, so he does.'

'It's very foolish to give trouble to a king,' said the big man. 'Now tell me, what's your name?'

'I am Gwynn, the fourth son of Rhys of Pembroke ... who are you?'

Gwynn's courage had returned since neither he nor Wuff looked likely to be eaten. The question amused the big rough man because he permitted a glint of fun to cross his face again.

'I am Dermot, the son of Donncha, the son of Murrough, and I am a king. You may not believe that, of course. For the time being it does not matter. I have a boy your age and a girl a bit older. These are my soldiers who are with me. Some of them are a bit rough. Some do not wash ... some even stink to heaven. But as soldiers go they are all right.'

His mind then seemed to stray, because he spoke almost to himself: 'Strongbow a beggar? If the boy knows that, then the dogs in the streets know it. A beggar! But who has sharper wits than a beggar? Or a greater hunger?'

He turned to Gwynn again: 'Tell me more about this man Strongbow. Where is he?'

Gwynn now felt very important, for only he knew the answers to the questions, and if the man who asked them was really a king in disguise it made him more important still.

'Strongbow now lives in a wreck of a castle at Striguil and my father said he would skin a frog for money,' Gwynn replied. 'My father said that no other knight will

9

go near him or help him because he is unlucky, but do you know what he said as well? He said that he is the best swordsman of all the Normans in Wales. I know that when he comes to Pembroke all the rowdies keep out of his way, and if anyone even told him to his face he was a beggar he would kill him stone dead.'

Dermot, the man who said he was a king, stroked his beard and then called out:

'O'Regan!'

A young man, better dressed than the others, came up to him from amongst the soldiers and Dermot said to him:

'Give this boy a coin. He has saved us three days' travel.'

Then he spoke to O'Regan in Irish. Gwynn knew some Irish, for Pembroke was the great port of departure and arrival, used by Welsh soldiers hired to fight in Ireland, and by Irish soldiers coming to fight in Wales and England. Races of soldiers were always passing through and buying provisions, so the town knew many languages.

O'Regan gave Gwynn a valuable Viking coin which made him splutter with gratitude, but O'Regan only laughed and then took him a little apart as if to tell him a secret. He spoke better Welsh than his master.

'Gwynn,' he said, 'my master, Dermot the King, really is a king, a very important king in Ireland. We are here on a serious mission, but that can wait. My name is Maurice O'Regan and I'm what you might call the King's manager. I supply him with information, help him to make up his mind about orders, and when he makes an order I see to it that it is carried out. It's a very interesting job and I'm always on the look out for helpers. Of course, the helpers have to be clever. Dermot the King likes you. He thinks you are very clever. As a matter of fact he said to me that you might, I said *might*, be a possible helper. I'll tell you what we'll do. We'll be here for the night. Come back later and tell us all the news about Pembroke. We want to know everything. And there might be another coin to jingle.'

When Gwynn went home for his supper and told his family what had happened, everyone in the house laughed.

'Another yarn from Irish liars and rogues,' his mother said.

'He's a king,' defended Gwynn.

'King indeed!' his mother went on. 'The last time Dermot the King of Leinster in Ireland came here, back in the early sixties, the sun shone around his shoulders. The cut of his clothes, the harness of his big white horse and the dress of his bodyguard would take your breath away, and he flung coins around to the crowd like thistledown.'

'Did your king give you any coins?' Gwynn's big brother Dai asked.

Gwynn thought it better to keep this information to himself lest there be a fight or he might have to hand it up.

'I have been promised coins,' he said cautiously.

Another roar of laughter from around the hearth.

'The Irish would promise you moonshine for midday! What do they want?' his brother Llewellyn asked.

'Important information,' retorted Gwynn with great dignity.

More laughter and derision echoed around the

kitchen and Gwynn's father remarked, 'I hope you haven't given them information of any good because if you have they'll be gone to rob or plunder and you'll never see them again.'

Gwynn hastily finished his supper and ran out of the house to loud cheers, with Wuff barking behind him. They ran like the wind down the long streets of houses and taverns towards the castle of Pembroke. Its massive bulk stood up against the sky as if to defy thunderbolts, let alone mortal man, and the long battlements showed a flurry of activity, with sentries looking over into the street, then to the harbour, then disappearing. From the highest turret flapped the battle standard of Henry the Second, King of all the Normans.

But of the man who said he was a king or his men there was no sign. Gwynn suddenly felt a bitter sense of disappointment because a strange thing had happened to him. He liked the big gruff man and he hoped that he really was a king. As for being hired as one of his helpers he had been excited out of his mind. Were they really all liars and rogues?

He paused in front of the great castle gates. Not a human being was in sight. Then Wuff, who had been circling around him, caught a scent. He barked in discovery, scurried down the street to the corner of the stone battlements, then down the steep hill at the side of the castle, still barking like mad. Gwynn raced after him, rounded the next corner of the great fortress, and found himself down against the mud flats and the low harbour inlet. From there the castle looked mightier still against the sky.

Suddenly, there were the Irishmen, forty of them gathered together, the big King with the grey hair in the

12

middle, O'Regan beside him. They all looked cross, very cross. Wuff barked and the big King looked up abruptly, his face full of anger and bushy eyebrows. He turned his eyes towards Gwynn and as he did the black rage vanished from his face and was replaced by a gleam of delight. He waved an arm high above his head.

'Here is the very man I want,' he cried. 'Come here! I want a loan of your brains.'

Gwynn went up to the King, bursting with importance. He could not hide his joy and relief that his real live king was still there as he said he would be. He went straight up to him with a grin as broad as a saucer of milk.

'Well, boy,' the King said in a loud voice. 'Here you are again, when men were never worse wanted. Tell me this now and tell me no more ... about how many men are in Pembroke Castle? Fighting men, I mean. Count up in your head and take your time. There's no need to be exact but I'd like to know how many there are ... if I wanted to bring them wine or ale or something like that ... as presents.'

Gwynn had no trouble with the question, for his father had often spoken of the amount of trade the castle created in Pembroke.

'There is a standing garrison all the time of 148 men on guard duty and there are upwards of 500 knights and foot soldiers at the ready for call up if needed, just for garrison work. And what's more,' continued Gwynn, 'there are servants and cooks to the number of thirty four in the castle as well. The chief cook is the same size and weight as a horse and my father says he would drink Milford Haven dry if he was left alone, and another thing...'

13

MacMurrough put his hand across Gwynn's mouth.

'Hold your tongue, boy,' he said, 'until we draw together our scattered wits. You have said enough for the time being. If what you say is right, and mind you I believe you, I think you have the makings of a first-class helper — isn't that right, O'Regan? Well, if you're right, and I'm not stupid, I would say that the men in that castle are very well contented, well paid and well fed, and that they would not dream of leaving it to take up other jobs, as soldiers anywhere else would. Am I right in my thinking, boy?'

'Red-hot spears would not drive them out. Every man in Wales wants their jobs. They are the only soldiers in the world who are not in danger of getting even a scratch,' Gwynn declared with a flourish. 'They are in the pay of King Henry, just holding the castle and Pembroke for him.'

As quickly as he had shown a smile, MacMurrough scowled.

'No good, blast their living guts,' he snarled. 'We are wasting our time. God help us, we're wasting our time — and I have no time. Full-bellied drones won't fight, not for any money. The only men who will fight are men who are jumping up and down in the air with the dint of the hunger.'

The rough men around the King murmured in support.

'What we want, MacMurrough,' O'Regan said, 'are men who are as desperate as cornered rats.'

The King spoke half to himself, half to the boy:

'Gwynn of Pembroke, of the great speeches and the brains, I have had letters of support from the same King Henry, urging his able-bodied subjects to enlist in my army in order to cure a little disorder which occurred in my land. And do you know what I might just as well have displayed in Devon or Bristol, England or Wales, when I was recruiting men?'

'I do not, Your Majesty,' said Gwynn properly.

'Do not call me "Your Majesty", the King said. 'In Ireland the ruler is known and addressed by his name. I am The MacMurrough. I am the Chief of my race and nation. I am addressed, and you may so address me, as "MacMurrough" ... now, where was I?'

'You asked me what you might as well have displayed in England and Wales as King Henry's letters?'

'Oh, yes,' MacMurrough recalled. 'I might just as well have displayed a head of cabbage. I have only four men ... four volunteers out of thousands who jeered at me. Three cutthroats and one gentleman! One from a Bristol gallows, a dullard from Devon, a Norman half-wit, and a Flemish knight called De la Roche. I am at the end of my rope.'

He shuddered in the chilly evening breeze. For some reason that he could not explain, Gwynn was sorry for him and pity oiled his mind.

'MacMurrough,' he cried. 'There *are* hungry men to be found, men who are out of work and mad for fight.'

The King shrugged and said only one word, 'Where?'

Gwynn was excited for he knew exactly what he was talking about.

'At Striguil Castle!' he shouted. 'Strongbow and all his men are in disgrace with King Henry. They would not have had full or contented feeds for months. One of them hanged himself the last full moon and my father said it was not madness but the hunger. They are desperate. They would tackle anything.'

MacMurrough the King inhaled fresh life. Of course! Strongbow! Strongbow the bankrupt, driven like a badger into the wet valleys of Wales to forage like an animal. The one time mighty Lord of Pembroke whose life and sword were now at robber level. The more MacMurrough thought, the more scheming plans contested the space inside his head. He whispered to Gwynn:

'Well done, boy! You have brought me nothing but luck.'

Then he roared to his men, 'Striguil tomorrow by noon, men. This might be your last week in Wales, but don't do any mischief tonight in Pembroke!'

Turning to Gwynn, he said, 'I would like you to come with me, for the fun, to Striguil. You could help me. Would you like that?'

Gwynn could hardly refrain from cheering.

'Yes, yes, I could leave now,' he cried, but MacMurrough ordered O'Regan to go to Gwynn's home with him to get his parents' permission. O'Regan was a quiet and gentle man and so reassured them fluently in their own Welsh tongue that they were satisfied to allow Gwynn off for the next day with people who, at first, they had thought to be a band of cutthroats.

Gwynn couldn't sleep a wink that night. He was up at dawn and had Wuff up and out as well. He raced so fast down the hill to the Irish camp that he almost landed head first into the mud flats. But the Irish soldiers were all still asleep.

There was but one human being astir. Dermot the King stood alone on the stone bridge across the inlet, looking out to sea towards Ireland and his dreams. He was wide awake. Gwynn went over to him and announced:

'MacMurrough, we are here!'

Dermot the King acted as if he knew Gwynn was there all the time and did not greet him in the usual way. His first words were:

'You are going to help me then?'

'Yes, we are,' said Gwynn firmly.

'Good! That's very good! I need a pair of extra eyes and ears, especially ears. In Norman castles here in Wales, they switch their speech from French to Latin, from Latin to Welsh, like the cackle of women at a wake. You can help me because you're from Pembroke and you're used to it. I want to know everything that is being said, even in whispers. Can you help me?'

'Your troubles are over, MacMurrough,' Gwynn replied. 'You can depend on me.'

The king thought and brooded a while.

'Can you keep a secret, boy?' he asked.

'I certainly can! Upon my grandmother's grave, I swear,' said Gwynn promptly.

'This is a terrible secret. If you tell anyone else about this secret, you will bring down upon yourself the king's curse — the worst curse in the world. Do you know what a king's curse is like? It means that until the day you die, you will never have good luck. Your three stomachs will sicken every day and your bowels will turn into liquid. Your milk will turn sour at every meal. Your meat will have maggots. Hair will grow on the palm of your right hand, like a beard. And that's only the half of it....'

Wuff lay down and put his paws over his eyes.

'I swear never, ever, to tell a single Christian, not even my mother,' said Gwynn, most impressed at the size of a king's curse, not even the half of which he had been told.

'All right then, I will tell you....' Dermot the King

17

sighed, stroking his beard. 'I have been betrayed by enemies and robbed and hunted, worse than even Strongbow. The only difference is that my kingdom was vast and rich, with cities and harbours, food, hunting and gold, great abbeys and castles. Now I must get men to fight for me to get back my kingdom, men who will fight alongside my own soldiers at home. Today we march to meet Strongbow ... and today I have not got enough pay to hire twenty foot soldiers.'

A great idea burst into Gwynn's brain box. 'Why not give them farms or a city instead of money? Strongbow's men would take anything.'

The gloom about the desperate King did not go away.

'The only land I have to give away is partly bad and wet. Briars and rushes are the best crops. The other part of the land I have is cursed and haunted by the drowned and robbed. The only cities I have are managed and owned by the Vikings, and they are fortified by great walls and towers ... Dublin, Wexford, Waterford.'

Gwynn wished he had a beard himself to stroke, but the notion passed swiftly as an even greater thought crossed the borders of his mind.

'MacMurrough,' he asked, 'how would Strongbow or his men know the land was wet or cursed? How would they know the Vikings occupied the cities? They would not know unless you told them!'

The big King's eyes blinked and a curious change came over him, gradually, slowly, a change just like the first trickle of water on to the wheel of a water mill. The big wheel starts to turn, very slowly at first, then as the water increases it goes faster and faster, until at last the whole mill roars with noise because all its parts are working.

So it was with Dermot the King's face and body. After a few seconds, Gwynn's words began to work the mill of his mind and the great gears began to move until at last his head was filled by a torrent. His face changed from gloom to blank. Then a glint appeared, his eyes smiled, then he gave a little laugh. That was followed by a waterfall of laughter. His whole body shook and he took Gwynn by the two hands, shaking both of them, with Wuff barking and jumping, and he, the King, not able to stop laughing, while tears of merriment danced on his face.

His men, now aroused, ran up to him but he brushed them away, saying:

'It's all right! Leave me alone! Make yourselves ready for Strongbow!' Laughter. 'Strongbow the hungry!' More laughter. Then finally he wiped his eyes, 'By heavens, there's a great lad here! If he stays with me, he will go far in the world. Come on, Gwynn, let us go and see what Strongbow has for dinner.'

The castle of Striguil looked motheaten, even at a distance. Mangy hens scratched outside it and hungry cur dogs scavenged for scraps. Their bald patches and greyhound ribs made Wuff appear like a prince.

Gwynn, comfortably riding with O'Regan on his horse beside Dermot the King, had had a long and interesting chat on the journey. He showed the party two short cuts which reduced the marching time by hours. Indeed the king declared they could not have managed without him at all.

As they came near the castle there sounded an alert. Dogs and look-outs had spotted the approaching party, and there was a furious fuss for a few seconds as men hurried from huts to get into the castle, strapping swords to themselves. Finally, the dogs were all whistled inside the crumbling outer walls and the last men shut and barred the gates. The shabby flag on the battlements indicated that Strongbow, Earl of Striguil, was inside.

Now the Irish were within an archer's range of the battlements. Dermot MacMurrough called forward two men, one of whom, O'Nolan, had a special life-long function which was to proclaim the authority and the indentity of his king. The second man the King named was the Flemish knight who had joined them, De la Roche. He was to go forward with O'Nolan in case there was a language problem because, apart from official pronouncements in Latin which he had learned by heart, O'Nolan spoke only Irish. As O'Nolan came past the King, MacMurrough stopped him.

'I want you,' he whispered, 'to give Strongbow his full set of titles — make it sound as important as you can!'

O'Nolan smiled and trotted forward with De la Roche.

As they waited, Dermot the King, obviously deep in thought about Strongbow, said to Gwynn, 'He was married when I met him last. A nice girl, too. Have they a family?'

'They have one son named Richard, but his wife is dead. From hardship and shame, my mother said.'

Dermot seemed visibly jolted and he made a strange reply.

'Yes, my boy, men must work and women must weep.'

The two horsemen were now being challenged at the

castle gates, whereupon O'Nolan roared with a mighty bellow, twice:

'Greetings to Richard, son of Earl Gilbert, known as Strongbow, *Rightful* Earl of Pembroke, and Earl of Striguil.'

The greeting struck a warm note, for at once the sentry on the battlements called back in French:

'Who greets the Rightful Earl of Pembroke?'

O'Nolan replied, and for the first time Gwynn was able to hear the titles of the big king named Mac-Murrough who sat so commandingly on the horse next to him:

'Greetings from Dermot, son of Donncha, son of Murrough; King of Uí Chinsealaigh, King of Leinster and the Norsemen; King of all Southern Ireland, and also of Meath.'

Dermot turned and gave a sidelong nod to Gwynn who was watching him intently, saying in Welsh:

'That is the way it was. That is the way it must be again.'

Within minutes the gates of Striguil Castle were thrown open and Gwynn watched in growing wonder as he recognized the Norman knight in battle armour who strode forward. It was none other than Strongbow himself! Dermot the King got down from his horse and walked towards him. No one else followed. The two men, king and earl, met, looked at one another and then embraced, hugging each other. Dermot remounted and beckoned to his men to follow him into Striguil Castle.

Gwynn could feel the pride and excitement mounting within him. Win or lose, he was about to take part, an important part, in the greatest adventure of his life.

## 2 The Promises

O'Regan spurred his horse and the whole group of Irish warriors moved toward Striguil Castle as one man. Inside the gates, they were stared at. Women gave them sullen looks while dogs, skinny bald dogs, whimpered. The soldiers were in battle dress and armour but there was none of the shine and colour that might have reminded Gwynn of King Henry's guards at Pembroke. Instead there were but tattered rags and rusting mail, as if the wearers had neither the energy nor the interest to look like soldiers. They were all thin and wiry, suspicious and cross looking.

Strongbow and Dermot the King were nevertheless talking excitedly to one another like long lost brothers. Could it be that they each saw in one another the means of their own survival?

Noting Gwynn on horseback with O'Regan, Strongbow asked, 'Is that fine boy your son Conor?'

'No. He's our horse tender,' said Dermot. 'A great boy. He speaks horse language! His name is Gwynn and he is able to tell me what the horses think. That's my chief adviser, Maurice O'Regan, with him. He is able to tell me what men think — sometimes.'

As Dermot's men on horse and foot examined the shabby outer yard with its stench of pigswill, Gwynn was surprised to hear his new master get down to business openly before everyone, while the dust was still on their clothes.

'Strongbow, rightful Earl of all Pembroke,' MacMurragh said, 'I want you to come back to Ireland with your men, to fight for a better life than this.'

Gwynn thought Strongbow would have accepted the offer on the spot. He did nothing of the sort. Instead, he gave a bellow of laughter:

'What's wrong with our life? We have a great life here! Yes, and it will be better when Henry's whelp dies of chicken-pox. But let's hear your tongue, Mac-Murrough! Let us sit down and enjoy a civil meal and a talk. We have all got hard bellyaches.'

To Gwynn's amazement, Strongbow was giving the impression that all was a life of cosy sunshine in Striguil. He ordered a feast to be made ready, but to the women he gave a savage hiss in French, an order that is only given in battle when all is lost and slaughter is on the menu. What he snarled from the side of his mouth sounded like *Shoff kee poh* but Gwynn knew that it meant *Run for your life*. The women scattered as if they had been whipped and soon the business of cooking a great meal was under way — in a castle where Gwynn firmly believed everyone was starving. He would have to keep eyes and ears open!

His mind was diverted from the wonder of it all by the arrival with Strongbow of a boy, the same size and age as himself.

'There's a new friend for you, Richard,' Strongbow said to his son. 'His name is Gwynn, and if you stay with him he will show you how to talk to horses!'

Strongbow's son Richard was very shy and did not say anything at first. However, when Gwynn whispered to him that he really knew nothing about horses but plenty about rat-hunting dogs and that Wuff was a champion ratter, he became a friend within minutes.

Soon the smell of cooking started to seep through the castle stones, turning their minds to the feast ahead. MacMurrough's men began to smile with relish, for they were all starving after the long march.

'Smells good, Pembroke,' said MacMurrough, never losing a chance to flatter Strongbow and fan the fury.

'Yes, it smells like heaven,' O'Regan sniffed appreciatively. 'Any dish we know about?'

'It's a mixture of fresh meats, a very old French concoction which was developed during the first crusade. I think you'll like it. It's given extra bite because the cooks add fresh vegetables to the cauldron and boil up the whole lot for about an hour. By heavens, MacMurrough, I declare it would bring the dead to life. Come on! Get your men seated and we will hear more of your plans.'

Strongbow was giving the lie to the rumours that he was a beaten, broken, starving pauper, with this show of feasting, just like it had been in the days of power. He was known to be very generous.

Strongbow had a ruddy complexion and a face smothered in freckles. He was tall in build with a short bull's neck packed with muscles. But his features were soft, like a girl's almost, and he had a weak voice. It gave his enemies a wrong impression — but many who thought he would fight like a girl never lived to tell the story. In his younger days he had been mocked for his courtesy and teased because he was a dandy. Now in his forties, the downfalls of life from his years of grace had razor-sharpened his mind to cunning.

Gwynn and Richard sat at one end of the top table, six places away from Strongbow and Dermot. Wuff lay hidden under the table, growling discontent now and then at some secret known only to himself. Gwynn kept his ears sharp about him for his was a most important task. He was MacMurrough's secret eyes and ears.

Strongbow was the perfect master of the feast and spoke without a care in the world. Gwynn, who knew MacMurrough's troubles, was afraid that his new master would fail miserably at this last chance to find soldiers.

'Ireland is a fair country, I have to admit, MacMurrough,' opened Strongbow. 'But for me or my men to go there, the rewards would have to be good. As you see, we have everything we want here. Not as good as other years of course, but then things are bad everywhere. Then there is our busy little King. A busy, nosey, inquisitive little man who would think at once that we were setting up a rival effort — a new independent business at his back. He would smell a new kingdom, just as happened in Sicily. And I tell you, Mac-Murrough, that waspish little man would laugh at me hanging by the neck from a royal scaffold.'

MacMurrough produced the first of his trump cards.

'O'Regan,' he called, 'give the rightful Earl of Pembroke the letters bearing the seal and sign of Henry the Second, King of England, Duke of Normandy and Aquitaine.'

MacMurrrough's harsh bellow rang around the hall with a flourish. Talk stopped as O'Regan produced the well-aired parchment. MacMurrough, with a majesty of gesture, laid it before Strongbow who opened it and read, half out loud, half to himself:

'Henry, King of England, Duke of Normandy and Aquitaine, Count of Anjou, to all his liegemen, English,

Norman, Welsh and Scots, and to all nations subject to his sway, greeting. Whensoever these letters shall come unto you, know that we have received Dermot, King of Leinster, into our grace and favour. Wherefore, whosoever, within the bounds of our territories shall be willing to give him aid as our vassal and liegeman, in recovering his dominion, let him be assured of our favour and licence in that behalf.'

Strongbow put the parchment down.

'At long last he has gone mad. How did you get him to sign *that*?' he said slowly, almost in disbelief.

'I sent him an army of my men and Vikings from Dublin to put manners on North Wales four years ago. He owed it to me,' replied MacMurrough.

A great black cauldron of the most deliciously smelling brew was wheeled out before the tables. The serving women were flushed with pleasure, and curtsied

with smiles. Their cooking has been a great success. Soon the Irish King and his men were diving into helpings of what looked like an Irish stew of Norman variety. There were pieces of white meat, morsels of pink meat, little slicelets of liver, miniature legs of rabbit or game. It did not matter; the concoction from the crusades was mouth-watering.

'Delicious! Delightful!' declared MacMurrough. 'Your women will have to tell me what is in it, for I must get my own women to prepare it at home. It is so good, Strongbow, it is no wonder you have the freckles. Tell me, what is it?'

'Never mind the contents,' laughed Strongbow. 'Enjoy the flavour.'

As the pace of eating the delicate meats slowed up, belches resounded through the great hall.

'I might be tempted to join you, MacMurrough ... I say *might*...' muttered Strongbow during a lull, 'but it boils down to this. How do you expect to pay us ...well ... properly? And for what?'

MacMurrough thought for a while, obviously coming to terms with the fact that he was not dealing with a half-starved penniless outcast any more. The wages would have to be good.

'I would need you to organize and transport across to me,' he began slowly, 'a trained army of not less than two thousand men. I am offering to you as wages two entire baronies of land, rivers and seas, south of Wexford. I am also offering to you, as wages, the cities of Wexford, Waterford and Dublin, which, as you know, is the biggest and wealthiest city in the western world.'

Gwynn was straining his ears to hear the exchanges, but Wuff was making it difficult. Right through the meal he had whimpered, once barking so loudly that Gwynn had to give him a kick, wondering if there was a ghost or a hare in under the table as well as the dog.

Strongbow was the only Norman at the table and did the bargaining on his own. His men ate elsewhere. He himself had eaten nothing, saying that he suffered from the 'crusader's curse', dysentry, on that day. Despite the offer of possessions he could never have dreamed of in his whole life, he carried on as if he knew that Mac-Murrough was on his knees and that he, Strongbow, was the man with the power. He wanted the last drop of blood, reducing the Irish King to beads of terrible sweat. His replies and smiles were those of a man as rich and powerful as the Sultan of Baghdad.

'All very fine, MacMurrough, all very fine, most generous ... but then these possessions are only for the time being. They have to be taken, held and defended. Look at your own case. Three years ago, you were the second most powerful man in all Ireland, the next High King many said, and the living High King's favourite and ally. All gone inside a year. Treachery and thieves are everywhere. No security! What can you offer me that will protect me and my men? What can you offer me, here and now, that will last forever?'

So Strongbow had the measure of the man he was talking to. He knew everything. He knew Mac-Murrough was on his knees!

Gwynn watched and listened as Dermot the King suffered, and as Strongbow talked on and on as if he were the happy owner of the western world himself. He listed his possessions and prospects in Wales, his web of blood connections across England, reaching right into the interior of France. He reminisced about battle tactics and campaigns, great victories, and great vaults of family treasures. Gwynn saw and heard it all, knowing that although Dermot kept up a brave show of interest, inside the big man's body there was nothing now but empty air.

Before Gwynn could hear the next exchange between the two leaders, Wuff climaxed a long low growl with a frenzy of barks. He shook himself free of Gwynn's feet and set off at speed down the stone halls towards the kitchens. Terrified, Gwynn got up and ran after him, but no one paid much attention to him because he was only a boy. All eyes were on the two leaders, while the women servants were busy going in and out serving those who had any room for more of the savoury meats.

Wuff ran with his nose to the ground, with Gwynn charging after him. He burst out into the sunlight of the great yard and galloped at speed through the door of an outhouse. Gwynn was at his heels when the greatest shock of his life pierced through his eyes and into the dead centre of his brains!

There in the middle of the outhouse floor was a huge mound of fresh rat pelts, hundreds of them. Next to that was a smaller heap of cat pelts, all fresh and newly skinned, and beside them a number of dog pelts of all sizes. The succulent stew consumed with gusto by Gwynn, MacMurrough and his forty men had consisted of rat, cat and dog flesh, killed, skinned and boiled inside an hour at Strongbow's savage hiss, *Shoff kee poh!* Gwynn's stomach revolted as Wuff burrowed into the middle of the rat pelts but so great was his terror that he swallowed hard. Above all, he thought of his master's plight. He had to get back quickly with the news.

He had been right! It was *Strongbow* who was the

29

beggar! *Strongbow* who was as poor as the rats, cats and dogs he had killed for the feast! He must be desperate.

Gwynn grabbed Wuff, slammed and locked the door of the outhouse and ran back to the great hall where Dermot the King instantly used his entrance to change the subject under discussion.

'Well, there you are, Gwynn! Where did you go? Was it a troop of horses or a ghost you were after?' MacMurrough turned to Strongbow. 'A very bright lad, a fine companion for your boy Richard.'

Gwynn had to think fast and so he did. He pretended to stutter an excuse while scolding Wuff and then he uttered a sentence in the simple Irish nearly all the ordinary people back in Pembroke knew.

'Tá an fear láidir ana bhocht!' He said it twice, quickly, like a flash. 'Tá an fear láidir ana bhocht!' (The strong man is very poor.)

The only sign his master gave that he understood was a slight tremor and twinkle in his left eye. Otherwise he carried on his conversation in the same manner, as if he had heard nothing.

'Yes, my dear Pembroke,' continued the Irish King, 'I can well understand your fear. Of course, something which will last forever is of great importance and I will not be small in my rewards to you ... if you will provide me with the forces I need, and provided The Mac-Murrough returns to ruling power. All Ireland power is not outside my hope. My great-grandfather did it and I am going to follow in his footsteps. Now then, let us see. What in the world lasts longer than royal blood? No man can steal that. They can beggar a royal, no doubt of it, but the blood line cannot be stolen, replaced or exchanged and it lasts to the end of time.'

He rose to his feet.

'Men,' he said, 'I want you to listen. I want you, and Richard, rightful Earl of Pembroke and Earl of Striguil, to hear and understand my words before the world.' He turned to Strongbow. 'In return for your help, I will bestow upon you after your arrival with your soldiers in Ireland the hand of my eldest daughter, the Princess Aoife, in marriage.'

Thunderous applause and happy laughter greeted this promise of wonder, but Gwynn was petrified. Mac-Murrough must not have understood that Strongbow was tricking him. He felt like screaming but Mac-Murrough continued in a solemn boom of voice:

'I further offer to Richard, Earl of Pembroke, the throne of Leinster after my day.'

More cheers and laughter from his Irish soldiers greeted this mighty and historic gesture. Gwynn felt like crying. His help had come to nothing. MacMurrough had not received the hidden information. To a man like Strongbow with nothing, not even enough ordinary food, Dermot the King had given away all that he owned in the world.

Gwynn walked away from the main body of MacMurrough's satisfied men, none of whom, not even MacMurrough, knew what their full bellies were fed on. He sat on a stone with a sad head in his hands. Wuff stood on his hind legs with his paws on Gwynn's lap so that he could lick his face and cheer him up. Gwynn was very downhearted when his dreams were interrupted by a familiar voice.

'Well done, boy. Well done! You saved more than a life today.'

Gwynn looked up, trying to hold back a tear. 'You spoiled everything, MacMurrough. You gave them everything and he was only tricking you. He has *nothing*. Do you know what you were fed on? You were fed on *RATS!* ... because that is all he had to feed us with. I saw the skins. A mountain of rat skins.'

'There now, boy,' said the King. 'Always keep your heart up, even when your head is under the water. I got your message. I knew you had found him out. Did you not hear my words immediately after?'

'I did,' said Gwynn. 'And it was awful. You gave everything away.'

'No, no, no, no, no, not at all,' said Dermot. 'Did you not hear my men cheer and laugh?'

'Yes?' said Gwynn doubtfully.

'Let me tell you something now. Another king's secret to be kept. It is not in my power to give Strongbow my kingdom. To be a king in Ireland, you must be of royal blood. You must be then *elected* king for your own small home kingdom and *then* you have to battle your way against all comers in order to rule Leinster. If you want to go from there to rule all Ireland, then you must tackle four other strong kings who have the same idea. I would have a better chance of turning Strongbow into a badger than I would of turning him into a king. Another little thing. We don't have thrones. We have inaugral stones.'

'What about his new wife, your own daughter, and she was not even here when she was promised away ... to a *beggarman*!'

'Watch your tongue, child!' exclaimed Mac-Murrough in mock horror. 'A military commander of many campaigns, if you please, not a *beggar!* Don't disturb my heart! Besides, we have different rules in our country. Here in this country Strongbow would take a wife and she would be a wife forever. In Ireland a marriage only continues if *both* the couple *want* it to continue. Do you see what I mean? A great system altogether.' He winked at Gwynn and Gwynn laughed at last.

'By the way,' said the happy King. 'We sail for Ireland at high tide in three days' time with an advance guard. Strongbow will come later but do you know what? He will send his son Richard over with us provided, and only provided, you come along as his companion. What do you say? I could do with you myself.'

Gwynn's heart nearly jumped out of his body.

'Yes, yes, MacMurrough, yes, I would love that, provided I can take Wuff. But what about my mother and father?'

'I think you can leave that to me and O'Regan,' mused Dermot the King. 'After all, I will be looking after you.'

He moved away from Gwynn to join O'Regan, but just as he joined him a sudden thought struck him. He turned around, licked his lips, juggled his stomach with his big hands and cried back to Gwynn:

'Very tasty those rats, weren't they?'

Gwynn spent the night before he left for Ireland listening to his older brothers.

'Wouldn't fancy Ireland much myself,' said Dai. 'Full of demons and snakes as well as witches.'

'I wouldn't mind that so much,' said Llewellyn, 'but what about the Fir Bolgs?'

'What's a Fir Bolg?' asked Gwynn with contempt.

'Ho, ho,' said Llewellyn. 'Dead keen to go to Ireland and he doesn't know what a Fir Bolg is. Everyone knows what a Fir Bolg is ... I suppose you don't know what a Banshee is either.'

Dai explained in a scholarly fashion: 'Fir Bolgs are half animal and half human. They have animal heads and human bodies and they live in the forests and the bogs. They feed on boys and girls whom they capture in their sleep at night. Ask anyone off an Irish ship.'

'Yes,' Llewellyn agreed. 'Very true ... and what about the Banshee and the Bow?'

Wuff growled and Gwynn snorted, 'There are no such things!'

'Ask one of the rogues you're going off with then,' said Dai. 'The Banshee is a woman ghost, and when she cries out from her fairy circle anyone who hears her dies roaring. The Bow is another demon, a cross between a lizard and a vampire, who crawls up on you in the dark and sucks your blood until you turn to seaweed. There are millions of them in Ireland ... just you wait and see!'

Next day there was a good wind and MacMurrough's ship prepared to sail. Gwynn and Wuff said good-bye to his mother and father, brothers and sister. He took his bundle of belongings on board with a strange feeling — and it *was* strange to be turning his back on Pembroke and its mighty castle. As sails and timbers creaked, the fair wind took them out to the deep swells of the Irish sea and the grey crags of Wales receded minute by minute. MacMurrough paced the deck, peering out to sea as if desire alone would bring his homeland closer. He seemed to have his mind on deep and dark thoughts.

When they were out of sight of land, Gwynn summoned up enough courage to ask him timidly, 'Is it true about the Bow?'

'What Bow?' MacMurrough's voice was bitter.

'The one that is half lizard and half vampire and sucks your blood at night,' said Gwynn.

MacMurrough knew at once that someone had been teasing the boy. He caught him gently by the two arms.

'Don't believe anything you hear about Ireland, especially about fairies and ghosts! The human beings are stranger than ghosts and demons. Yes, Gwynn, there is indeed a half lizard, half vampire that sucks blood, young blood, day as well as night. He is a human being, born of woman, though you wouldn't think it. His name is Tiernan O'Rourke, a mad malignant animal, a ruler of a small but important kingdom, Breifne. That man is my enemy, the reason why I was searching like a beggar for men from Aquitane to Pembroke. He or I must die, for there is a life of hate and blood and war between us. He brought me down. He is in my way on the way up, and worse still he has a helper. A tight-fisted goat of a king on my western flank — at my own back door — Fitzpatrick, King of Ossory. He has my young son Enna in chains as a hostage for my submission. I submit to the vermin or Enna is dead, or worse. That's what lies before us, you and I, Gwynn. And do you know what? We are going to get the better of them!'

MacMurrough the King paused and let Gwynn go. Gwynn looked out to sea with him, and as the soft hazy greens of Ireland and the blues of Mount Leinster appeared ahead, he swore to battle alongside him, win or lose.

# 3  A Secret Army

At about midday on the first of August, 1167, the ship carrying Dermot MacMurrough the King and its cargo of men, two boys and one dog, dropped anchor beneath the fort of Glascarraig. Glascarraig, with its lofty earthworks and church for travellers, was the port for Dermot's capital Ferns, fifteen miles inland.

From the first sighting of land, there had been moments of terrible tension. MacMurrough did not want to be detected and he was uncertain whether the lookout fort was still in friendly hands. It was only when they came close to shore that they could identify the distinctive MacMurrough emblem flapping aloft. This emblem consisted of two winged angels supporting a shield above and below, while the shield was supported on either side by two lions. The centre shield contained a lion above two moon crescents. When MacMurrough saw that sign of safe passage he beamed with excitement. There was a flurry of activity all over the ship as men grabbed their belongings. Gwynn and Richard, who had been at the prow watching the beaches and the deep green of the land ahead becoming more visible minute by minute, were suddenly interrupted. MacMurrough let out a mighty bellow:

'All men on deck! All men on deck! Men, boys, dog, and crew on deck!'

There was a powerful command in his voice and Gwynn fought to get out in front so that he could hear everything and watch the King while he was saying it. MacMurrough extended his mighty hand above his head.

'My faithful and gallant men,' then turning his eyes down to Gwynn, Richard and Wuff, 'and faithful and gallant followers! Listen to me! You have followed me without question in danger and in the dark. You have proved that you were prepared to die for me. You know where we have been. Now I am going to tell you where we are going, and I'm going to tell you *how* we are going to get there. First of all, we need rest and quiet. To plan! So we are going to hide. Go home to your wives as if you had never been away. Look after your crops. Tell no one anything, not even lies. De la Roche and his Flemish men will swop their gear for Irish clothes and they will train you at night. They know the battle tricks across the world, from the burning sand of Syria to the wet valleys of Wales. Do what they tell you to do!

'The next thing is this. You are *not* to talk about me. I am going into hiding in Ferns Abbey. *No one* must know I am back. If our enemies across the mountains in Ossory find out that I am back, we will be hunted down, destroyed, beggared, and I will be killed or, worse, blinded.'

Gwynn shuddered at the thought that there were worse ways to be than dead.

'Don't *mention* my name,' continued MacMurrough in a loud voice, 'but if there's a stranger about, *condemn* me. I will hide in Ferns Abbey until our hired help arrives from Strongbow, and when they do you are to be as good at the trade of war as they are. We will not move until we are strong, but when we are strong we will not be greedy. We will move forward, bit by bit, little by little, until we are great again. We will force the Vikings of Wexford and Waterford to their knees. Then Ossory, then all Leinster and Meath, then Dublin ... and you know what we will do with Bréifne!' He roared out the word like 'Brefneeee!'

The moment MacMurrough mentioned Bréifne, it was as if he had cast a wicked spell on his men, for their faces turned black with hatred. They let out a chorus of curses and yells the like of which Gwynn had never heard in his life before. Roars of 'Revenge! Revenge!' fanned out across the waves, and Gwynn was overwhelmed with a great curiosity as to what this revenge was about. When the roars died down, MacMurrough was nodding his head in agreement with a happy smile on his face, glad that he had stirred the blood in his men.

'Yes, men, I know how you feel. We will get Breifne! And after that, the High King....' he paused and finished after a second's dramatic silence with a ferocious roar, louder than the wind or thunder of waves on the surf, 'AND AFTER THAT, ALL IRELAND!'

The cheering lasted for ten minutes. Whenever it seemed it might stop, someone began another yell of excitement. Gwynn and Richard cheered like mad and Wuff barked and howled, nose in air, unhappy he could not bark louder. When they were all worn out cheering, the ship moved into shallow water where horses, baggage and men disembarked in safety.

MacMurrough disappeared, and when he reappeared there was a roar of laughter from his soldiers because he was clothed from head to foot in the black robes, cowl and belt of an Austin friar. He scowled for silence and from then on his men, including O'Regan, paid no more attention to him, as he had ordered. When they came up

from the beach into Glascarraig, O'Regan took command, but MacMurrough the King put Gwynn and Richard up on his own horse and he, the King in disguise, walked humbly alongside them in his big friar's sandals.

Gwynn had a great view of this new country, and if he

missed something on one side, Richard pointed it out from the other side. It was a lovely time of the year and the brown golden corn ears rustled against one another in the breeze. Cattle were fat and contented in their green paddocks and grazing lands, and the plaintive cry of sheep arose from great flocks. A couple of miles after passing a great cattle assembly called Boolavogue, Dermot MacMurrough's royal residence and seat of government came into view. The huge square castle dominated the countryside around, even over-shadowing the fresh stones of the great monastery with its round tower. The stone buildings — cathedral, churches and castle — were surrounded by a great many lime-washed houses with thatched roofs, sparkling white in the sun, which dotted the landscape like mush-rooms.

As they approached Ferns from the east, the King gave his instructions to Gwynn:

'You are to stay in Ferns Castle with my wife and family. Conor, my boy, will show you around, and you are to be specially nice to Aoife because she has her Daddy's temper. Then every day you and Richard, and of course Wuff, are to come to see me in Ferns Abbey. My lady wife will give you something nice for me in a basket. You will be able to bring me all the news and whatever messages O'Regan gives you. He will tell my family all about you so I think you will have a good time.

'One other thing — when I leave this company at the gateway of Ferns Abbey, take no notice! Do not say good-bye! I'm just an old monk returning from a jour-ney. Tell them in the castle that I will not be in Ferns for a few days. I want to give them all a special surprise tonight. Take care and say *nothing*!'

At the great gates of Ferns Abbey, Dermot turned sharp right and walked up to the heavy timber door, where he pulled the entrance bell as if he had been doing so all his life. Gwynn, Richard, O'Regan and the entire contingent of about fifty continued on up into the streets of thronged Ferns as if nothing unusual had taken place whatever. But before entering the market places, the whole body split up and most of the men vanished their separate ways. Only O'Regan and the strangers, Gwynn, Richard, De la Roche and his little group of Flemings, now dressed like ordinary Irish men, walked on, encountering the curious gaze of the people. On they went, through the main thoroughfare, up to the summit of the hill, until they arrived before the gates of MacMurrough's fortress. O'Regan was immediately admitted, the party entered, the gates slammed shut behind them and suddenly cries of welcome and excitement rang throughout the halls.

MacMurrough's Queen, Mor, raced down the great stone steps with fear in her face. Her two children, Conor, aged fifteen, and Aoife, aged eighteen, both very like their father, were bubbling with hope.

'Where is he? When will he be here?' they wanted to know.

'Is he alive?' was the question asked by Mor.

A crowd gathered around as word went throughout the castle. Servants, ministers, administrators, the great legal chief, O'Doran, and Fern's Bishop O'Haye wafted wondering into the hall, to greet the head of Mac-Murrough's government, Maurice O'Regan. Only Wuff's sharp bark of protest drew attention to the strangers with him.

To all pleadings, O'Regan insisted, 'He is safe and

well, but is now a pilgrim at, I think, St. David's. I will tell you all when I rest. He sent a message, and that is that you are to look after his friends here.'

O'Regan introduced Gwynn, Richard and Wuff and while he was explaining who De la Roche and his troop were, MacMurrough's son and daughter came around, tingling with curiosity about the newcomers. Gwynn and Richard were also thrilled at what promised to be an exciting mixture — an Irish prince and princess, the son of a Norman earl, an adopted Welsh boy and a dog genius. Conor MacMurrough was very much the man in his father's absence but he promised to show his new friends all the secrets of Ferns and the country as soon as they got used to one another's speech. For Richard this would take time because he had never learned Irish in his life and it was very different from his native language, French. Aoife was as beautiful in Gwynn's eyes as she was sweet and they took an instant liking to one another. Before dusk, Gwynn felt as if he had been there all his life and did not want to leave it ever.

After supper, a friar was announced to Queen Mor. He had a special plea from the Abbot of Ferns Abbey. An urgent royal conference was to take place in the Abbey that very hour and he requested the attendance of the entire MacMurrough family, along with the King's chief administrators.

Within half an hour the great abbey gates admitted the royal party including, at Conor's invitation and to their huge delight, Gwynn, Richard and Wuff. O'Regan, O'Doran, Bishop O'Haye and Mac-Murrough's chief recorder, MacCriffan, were there too, for they suspected that state and church business was in the powerful Abbot's mind. They were shown to the guest room and waited. Within minutes, a doddering old monk came in, wheezing and grunting. A bent old man, he was dusting and fixing things, getting in everyone's way and on everyone's nerves until the Queen very crossly dictated:

'Begone, friar! Bring the Abbot before us at once!'

At that curt order the old monk threw himself up into the air with a wild 'hurrooo', fired back his cowl and robes and shouted:

'Begone yourself, woman! It is myself, Mac-Murrough!' and he bellowed with laughter while he hugged them all, even his Queen who still pretended to be vexed. It was a mad sight for Gwynn who had seen so many strange things inside one week.

When the fuss subsided and those grave old servants, shaken by their ruler's gaiety and seeming lunacy, had gathered their wits, MacMurrough spoke to them, exactly as he had spoken to his trusted men on board ship. The plan of campaign was outlined. O'Regan was to be the chief administrator of the kingdom and its business, while he, Dermot, was to be hidden as if he were dead.

There was just one fresh order. MacCriffan was to keep him supplied with books from his great library, the collection made by MacCriffan himself, lest he lost his wits from boredom.

'I am not very good as singing psalms or reciting the monastery vespers,' he growled.

For Aoife he had some special news. He had a fine and nobel earl, Lord of Pembroke and Striguil, for her husband. A brilliant man, a soldier of fortune across the world, brave, generous, no boy with flaxen hair, perhaps, but if it didn't work out there was the Brehon

Law and they could part company.

'No!' declared Aoife, nose in air.

'That's my good spirited daughter!' chortled Mac-Murrough. 'Don't buy the bull calf until you've seen it trot! Well, there's time enough for that!'

And so, in great happiness, they parted from Mac-Murrough and returned home. Gwynn, Richard and Wuff had been given special quarters, high up in the castle, where they had a wonderful view of the country all around. They had a few days of rest and strolling about Ferns looking at the strange sights, the Holy Well of St. Aidan being one of the most mysterious.

'It's a very famous well with magic powers,' explained Conor MacMurrough. 'If you jump into that well in your skin on Christmas Eve, an hour before midnight, no sword or spear will kill you and you will never, ever, be killed by a weasel's spit, because as every fool knows a weasel's spit is poison.'

'Liar!' said Aoife.

'It's all very fine for you to talk. You don't have to fight and you are in bed on Christmas Eve, and it is well known weasels are afraid of women,' retorted Conor.

Richard, son of Strongbow, concluded that true or false, he would give it a try.

'I will jump into it on Christmas Eve, even if the big well is covered in ice,' he said.

Richard, though shy, was beginning to thaw. Usually very silent, whenever talk of war or battles or fights arose he turned into a man-eating chatterbox with a light in his eye.

'A splendid idea,' said Conor. 'But you won't have a chance because there are always thousands here trying to jump into the well every Christmas Eve and it only fits four men. The two of you are so small, you'd be killed.'

'I know what we will do,' said Gwynn. 'We will borrow forty barrels, fill them up with St. Aidan's water and rent them out on Christmas Eve!'

Many other great plans were discussed over the next few weeks and months as Gwynn, Richard and Wuff explored the great woods, the water mills, old monasteries, fairy rings and forts around Ferns. In the autumn they watched the men cut the corn, store the grain and brew ale from it. It was then that Gwynn and Richard learned something very important. The land all around Ferns was the richest in France, England, Wales or Ireland, and twice as much grain grew from it as in other places. That was why the MacMurroughs were so powerful and why they were so envied. They held the best lands in Ireland.

Gwynn and Wuff went to see the king disguised as a monk every day, going at different times so that no one would suspect anything. They always brought something tasty made in the castle kitchens, skilfully hidden by Queen Mor under a layer of vegetables. Gwynn needed to tell him very little about the family, for Mor visited him every week at dusk. Two things were of major concern to MacMurrough: Was his secret still safe? Were his enemies yet alert? Satisfied on both points, the next questions were about his army. Were his men being trained by De la Roche? Were they learning fast or not?

In the beginning Gwynn had explained that though De la Roche was doing his best, the numbers of men to be trained in secret were so great that it would have been impossible to do a large scale job without attracting attention. So with O'Regan acting as interpreter, De la Roche had picked the best of MacMurrough's men and trained them to train the rest in small groups. He showed them how to fight as the Normans did on the crusades and in Italy, doing away with the Irish custom of mass attacks in one big crowd rush and substituting tactics of attack from left and right. He also instructed them in the art of inviting an enemy force into a trap, and he greatly improved sword and spear play.

MacMurrough was delighted to hear all this from Gwynn, who was now both busy and important. He listened very carefully, grunting, 'Yes, yes, I see,' as he munched at a big apple tart.

One winter night, as it grew near to spring, he was unable to finish his pie and he gave a lump to Gwynn who saw that MacMurrough was becoming both pale from indoor life and fat from eating and inactivity. He was in a contented mood, however, and that night, for the first time, he told Gwynn about his early life and adventures.

'You know, Gwynn, I was not much older than you when I was made king of my people. My father was killed by the Dublin Vikings and they killed a dog and buried it with his corpse. We won't forget *that*, I can tell you! My eldest brother was killed the same year. My next brother, Enna, died in Wexford and that left only me or an infant. I was elected and, at once, before I had a chance to give one single order, the whole of Ireland turned on me, a soft thing. My men did the best they could but they were no match for the High King O'Connor. I was not good enough to lead them properly at the time. We were shamed and slaughtered; the two together!'

MacMurrough speared an apple with a dagger and the juice from his teeth crunched down the front of his black friar's habit. He picked up Wuff, placed him on the table to finish the pie, and then continued with the story, striding up and down the stone flags of the guest room.

'High King O'Connor did not come on that expedition himself. No! He had an animal to do the job instead. He sent a human scum, a sack of vermin with one eye, an insult to the name of ruler or law, and a heart's curse to the nature of the woman who carried him, called...'

His voice rang with fury, then dropped to a whisper when he uttered the name, as if he was afraid his own mortal tongue might not be able, in awful hatred, to form the words, '... Tiernan O'Rourke.'

'I don't like to tell you the worst of it, boy, but you might as well know some of it or you will not understand what I have to do. O'Rourke invaded my lands, and not contented with reducing me, a boy, to desolation, he decided to reduce my people to starvation. He marched right through Uí Chinsealaigh from top to bottom and came back along the sea coast burning, pillaging, killing men and cattle. He looked at me when I was caught as if I were a druid's changeling in a cradle. When I was brought before him, as the King, he laughed at me. He left me alive.'

He smiled but Gwynn knew it was not for fun.

'Did you ever get revenge?' he asked, hoping MacMurrough had cut O'Rourke's head off.

The King in the monk's robes nodded his head several times in glee. 'I stole the crab's wife away and every valuable and herd of cattle she possessed in the scab's bogs of Bréifne.'

'You did not,' cried out Gwynn, quite shocked at such a foolish revenge.

'I did so,' said the King. 'It took me some time, of course. Over the years we grew stronger. We planned carefully. No mad moves or anything like that. In the end, we were back to the strength of my father's time. I joined forces with the Ulster King and I made him High King of All Ireland. He was an enemy of O'Connor, of course, and his jack-ass O'Rourke, but O'Rourke went on to make one more bad mistake.'

'He stole the High King's wife?' queried Gwynn.

'Nothing as mad as that,' said MacMurrough. 'No! He stole a piece of good land belonging to his wife's family, the Kings of Meath ... lovely country. So there was an awful row. The High King ordered O'Rourke out. O'Rourke roared in fury like a mad bull driven off a green field full of daisies, and the High King left it to me to put manners on him.'

'You massacred him and his men and burned down the whole of Breifne,' said Gwynn, very excited at the thought of MacMurrough's revenge.

'God bless me, Gwynn,' MacMurrough said in mockery, 'but where do you bury all your dead? No! What would a long campaign to the North of Ireland do for me? Overland as well? It would lose men. No! Something delicious happened instead. The King of Meath, an old friend, sent down a message to me that his own sister, O'Rourke's wife, was sick, sore and tired of O'Rourke — the only thing that surprised me was that the grand little woman had not hanged herself years ago. He went on to say that she pleaded for me to rescue her from the old goat's clutches. I took my best men on the long journey. The King of Meath made the arrangements. I boldly knocked on the gates of Bréifne Castle, caught her and fired her up on horse back; and away we went. We took along with us every beast — horse, cow and bullock — we could lay hands on, all the way back to Ferns.'

MacMurrough laughed at the memory of a hilarious escapade, and kept on laughing, for he wasn't finished the story at all.

'Wait now, Gwynn,' he said, 'until I tell you the best of it. In this country when you do something like that you have to pay what's known as an honour price. Dervorgilla! Dervorgilla! That was her name.' He laughed again and slapped his thigh. 'The proper honour price for Dervorgilla which I should have paid O'Rourke was one hundred ounces of gold. A queen's ransom!' MacMurrough tittered. 'I never paid it!' Mac-Murrough bellowed with such laughter that Gwynn laughed as well, and Wuff barked.

'There he was, the crooked old crook, the bleary-eyed, scurvy, toothless lizard, with no cattle, no horses, no wife and, by heavens, no honour price!'

The tears of laughter streamed down Mac-Murrough's face. 'The whole country, north, south, east and west, burst its guts laughing at him, while he groped for swords and found nothing but ash plants.'

'Why didn't you cut his head off?' demanded Gwynn.

The laughter vanished abruptly from Mac-Murrough's face.

'That is the question, my boy. Why didn't I cut his head off? I'll tell you. Because at the same time a disaster took my mind off his head. Anyhow, I was certain he was as finished as a landed salmon. A revolt rose up against my ally the King of Ulster, whom we made High

King. He was killed, and our arrangements collapsed.

'Why didn't I cut O'Rourke's head off? I will never know. In any event my strength was halved. Rory O'Connor wanted to be High King, so he sent a great army to ruin me. He put O'Rourke in charge. Every friend I ever had saw their fate and left me, Irish as well as Viking. All I had was my own family and people. We hadn't a hope. When O'Rourke and O'Connor's hordes were at the outskirts of Ferns, I left to hire soldiers from the King of the Normans. I had seen them in action a few years before and I never saw anything like their battle tricks.

'So Gwynn, here we are, waiting for the fine weather and Strongbow's lean men, and me hiding in fear of my life.' MacMurrough pondered in silence. 'It's a miracle that no one has found out where I am ... or that De la Roche is here training my men.'

Gwynn and Wuff left him as usual, not realizing that the cosy days of visits and ramblings around Ferns were over. That very same week-end, a Flemish soldier, one of De la Roche's platoon, took time off to fish in a stream running through the lovely Blackstairs mountains. His breastplate of armour and his short sword were concealed by an Irish cloak as he whiled the warm day away. He was jumped by a search party of Fitzpatrick's, the king of neighbouring Ossory. In two days, his dead and tortured body was dumped outside a MacMurrough outpost. There was only one thing to be thankful for; he could only speak Flemish. Nevertheless, an armed foreign soldier in a suit of mail had been discovered. MacMurrough's game was up. In a matter of days, his enemies would be swarming to Ferns like locusts, and Strongbow's hired help was a sea away.

50

# 4   The First Battle

Gwynn raced as hard as his legs could carry him to Ferns Abbey with the bad news. The King's face grew black with rage when he heard it. When he recovered, he cursed so loud and long that monks flew in all directions like scalded cats. The monastery bell tolled out, then the cathedral bell, then the bell of St. Peter's. Soon every fighting man was running in alarm to Ferns. Mac-Murrough could not get his monk's robes off fast enough, so he ripped them to bits with his mighty hands and threw them out of the window in a black rag ball. He buckled on his great sword and bounded out through the gates, white with fright and fury. His men weren't fit enough yet to follow Banshees, let alone fight an army.

Dermot the King had not taken four strides outside the abbey gates when he was recognized.

'The King! The King!' the cry went up. 'Mac-Murrough is back!' The shouts echoed up the hill towards the busy market-place. The news spread like wildfire and before long, the old battlecry rose across the crowds, 'MacMurrough Aboo!' MacMurrough to victory.

The big King marched so fast through the crowd that Gwynn had to trot to keep up with him. Soon he was in the great market square before the castle, which was filled with stalls and traders, horses, cattle, fowl, pigs and sheep, ornaments and earthenware jugs — all mingled in a bedlam of noise. He walked through with an air of command that invoked silence and set geese squawking in alarm, until the fortress gates of his castle swallowed him.

Inside, he roared for men and attention. O'Regan and De la Roche reported at the gallop: 'No, they certainly were not able to take on all comers!'

MacMurrough's men were being well trained, it was true, but they were being specially trained to fit in with the Norman soldiers in an overall battle plan, and the Norman hired help had not yet landed in Ireland.

'What in hell's name am I to do?' yelled Mac-Murrough.

Gwynn had a brain hurricane.

'Pretend to be a crooked old crock like O'Rourke,' he whispered. 'If the High King comes, beg for peace for a few months and say that the Fleming was only a traveller from Pembroke and a poor orphan as well.'

'Did you hear that, men?' boomed a startled Mac-Murrough. 'Did you hear what came out of the boy's mouth? Upon my soul, if he was half grown up, or even a few inches higher, I would give him an army command! That is it, then. That's what we will do. We will steer whoever comes against us into the valley of Cillossna. We will go armed to the teeth but crying for mercy. I want all of you and all the men to look like death warmed up, no match even for a convent of nuns. I will go along with you in my grandfather's vest. I will get the boys to lead me. No one is to draw arms. You are to look as useless as old Granny Coreesks.'

Within three days the chain of outposts on the mountains reported the marching of an army against Uí Chinsealaigh from the north. The look-outs had no trouble in recognizing the leaders. They were the restored High King, O'Connor, and one other horror returned from the grave's edge, Tiernan O'Rourke of Bréifne. As they edged, by skirmishes and bush fires, into Cillossna's valley, it was seen that they had far too many swords and battle-axes for MacMurrough. They could wipe Uí Chinsealaigh out if they saw fit.

The two armies drew close to one another; the attackers a fiery alert force of fox-eyed men, the defenders looking like a yawning flock of dirty sheep. Gwynn was trembling with fear and excitement, not so much because he was helping MacMurrough, but because he was going to see and hear the scurvy tooth-less lizard he had heard so much about, Tiernan O'Rourke.

'Take a good look at O'Rourke,' said MacMurrough. 'He will be the one with the evil eye. Only the one eye. That one eye can turn milk to blood. If he looks you straight in the eye, turn your face away.'

Dermot MacMurrough was dressed in a long white robe yellowing with age and stains, torn at the hem. He creaked along as if in pain, leaning on a stout wooden staff, with one shoulder bent. He kept one side of his face and one eye up toward the sky, as if he had a crick in his neck. His hand was held by Gwynn who led him. He was propped up from behind by Richard, as if he might fall in an instant and break into bits.

The two columns of warriors met and the usual greet-ings, which preceded even a battle, took place. The High King's titles were shouted out by his chief noble-man at some length. He finished with a dry salute from 'Tiernan Mor O'Rourke, King of Bréifne, Lord of the Lakes and Passes of the North.'

'Bogs and swamps more likely,' whispered Mac-Murrough under his breath to Gwynn.

The High King's spokesman then offered insult to MacMurrough:

'Greetings to Dermot, son of Donncha, son of Murrough, *one time* King of Leinster,' and not another word or title.

As usual MacMurrough's hereditary master of ceremonies, O'Nolan, made to go forward to give his royal master, the King of Uí Chinsealaigh some vestige of dignity, but MacMurrough whispered hoarsely to him, 'Stay where you are! This is the day to kiss backsides.'

Then he turned to Gwynn and Richard: 'Take me forward and make sure I look like Famine and Black Death put together.'

The leaders of the invading force watched in amazement as the shambling figure of the once feared battle-master, MacMurrough, stumbled towards them. His arm shook as he waved a greeting. He seemed to totter and be saved from a fall by two grandchildren.

One man, however, did not believe his one eye — Tiernan O'Rourke. He got down from his horse and Gwynn caught his breath with terror. Wuff growled lowly at some invisible evil as O'Rourke walked slowly over, kicking a stone out of the way as if he wished it were MacMurrough's head. He was not the crooked old crock that MacMurrough had described. He was every bit as big as MacMurrough, broad, heavy, quick. But there was only an empty socket where his left eye had been and the whole scalp of his head above the socket was one large white scar where no hair grew. The cheek under the scar twitched all the time, while his other side face, with its half head of hair, gave the idea that he had two faces. But ugliness was not the most terrible thing about him. His one sliding brown eye swivelled above a vulture's beak and the cruelest slit of thin lips Gwynn had ever seen.

'Yes,' shuddered Gwynn to himself. 'He does have the evil eye. He would turn milk into blood.'

O'Rourke looked at MacMurrough and MacMurrough glanced up at him, while giving the appearance of the palsy.

O'Rourke then spoke in a gutteral growl: 'Well, vermin, is it the pox that ails you? I tell you, vermin, that if the High King of Ireland were not here, I would cure your pox for you for all time.'

'Forgive me, O'Rourke,' quavered MacMurrough, 'I have done you much mischief. Forgive me, I am not long for this world.'

O'Rourke stared in disbelief. Then he put his one eye on Gwynn and Richard.

'Fine, lovely little boys,' he growled. 'Wouldn't it be a great pity if any evil were to happen them?'

'We are at your mercy, Tiernan O'Rourke,' said MacMurrough feebly.

High King O'Connor could hardly believe the MacMurrough he saw before him. Here was a humble little man, long past his best, with no belly for argument or fight. This shuffling, mealy-mouthed Dermot was begging for peace without contest, wheezing that his strength was spent and that what little he had left would be wanted for his last pilgrimage to St. Patrick's Purgatory. His only desire was to be left in peace, to fish in the River Slaney and to count his beads with his grandchildren at night beside the fire. At this stage, MacMurrough tottered and took a little weakness. He would have fallen had not Gwynn and Richard rushed to his side, supporting him with great fuss and vigour.

The High King began to show concern, but O'Rourke's men smelt treachery. The feeling that they were going to go all the way back to the north of Ireland without loot, burning or treasure started to torment them. In a short while they decided to take things into their own hands. Without warning, some of them flung themselves on the nearest of MacMurrough's men.

'No! No,' bleated MacMurrough, who was now deep in flattery of the High King, but it was too late. As the two Kings were talking agreeably, battle was being joined in the front ranks.

It was too much for Strongbow's son, Richard. He shook himself from MacMurrough, screeched a French battle-cry and split the skull of one of O'Rourke's men with a rock, before being swept into the cauldron of battle. Gwynn's temper was fired and he jumped to join his friend in the fight, but MacMurrough, without showing the slightest muscle move to anyone, clasped his big hand around Gwynn's neck and held him paralyzed as if he were only a fly.

'Later, child,' he whispered weakly, 'later!'

MacMurrough's men were overwhelmed by weight of numbers, and when at last the outraged High King succeeded in parting the enemies, two hundred bodies, dead or wounded, littered the valley of Cillossna. The High King was very angry that his authority had been set aside and that battle should have started while peace was being arranged. To O'Rourke's sullen rage, he made the peace with the ghost of The MacMurrough who had known great power in the land. He recognized MacMurrough as King of Uí Chinsealaigh, provided he in turn recognized O'Connor as High King of All Ireland.

'Agreed, and blessings upon you, great King,' prayed MacMurrough.

There was one other condition. The honour price would have to be paid to O'Rourke for the theft of his wife Dervorgilla. One hundred ounces of gold, not one speck of gold dust less!

'Again I bless your wisdom, great O'Connor of Connaught. I gladly agree to repay Bréifne's ruler for my wicked deed in the past. I pray that the Lady Dervorgilla finds new rest and peace with her good husband, Tiernan.' MacMurrough blew his nose and wiped his brow before continuing, 'I also return, because of my sorrow, the cattle stolen from O'Rourke along with their increase in calves and may God forgive me!'

A spasm of coughing overtook him as he spoke the words. Gwynn made a great show of supporting him, but he knew that MacMurrough's fit of coughing had been brought about because his own words were choking him to vomit.

The peace arrangements and agreements were completed. MacMurrough had borrowed the time he urgently needed. With heart-bursting relief, he and his men watched the last of the High King's expedition leave the valley of Cillossna, staying there on the one spot with his hand on Gwynn's shoulder, watching until long after they had left the valley. He still pretended to be feeble in case any of their rearguard had stayed behind. Finally, the smoke signal from one of his secret outposts told him that the last man had gone well clear of the valley.

MacMurrough reached down, picked Gwynn up and

placed him like a vase of flowers on a rock out of the way. He then gripped his stout wooden staff and bellowing like a bull on fire, he lashed and smashed the nearest tree to bits, until nothing was left in his hand but the stump of his staff. He paused, exhausted. He turned toward the north and his raucous roar filled the valley. It was so loud a roar of pain and fury that it nearly bent the trees in echo.

'I will hang you, Tiernan O'Rourke, and burn you alive while you hang! Satan's black curse follow you, O'Rourke, as long as you live and after you die!'

He sat down on the rock where he had put Gwynn, heaving his chest with exhaustion. Before he could say another word, Gwynn jumped to his feet. Richard was nowhere to be seen.

'Richard!' Gwynn called at the top of his voice. 'Richard, where are you?'

Suddenly there was new panic. Richard, Strongbow's son, was missing. Gwynn ran to the place where the battle took place, calling all the time, followed by Mac-Murrough and a throng of men. Gwynn raged within himself that he had not gone into the battle with his friend, vowing that he would never forgive himself if anything was wrong. Soon it was seen that something had gone sadly wrong, for Gwynn gave a startled cry.

Half-hidden by the dead body of one of O'Rourke's men was the body of Richard, looking just as if he were asleep, with a knife wedged in his ribs. Dying, the battling Richard may have been, but he had taken his killer with him. He must have picked up a dropped dagger, for his fist still gripped the weapon he had driven into the Bréifne man. Gwynn was heartbroken to find his friend in adventure and games killed. If only he had been with him he thought, the two of them together could have killed his attacker before he got the upper hand.

'I should have gone with him,' cried Gwynn. 'Why did you not let me go with him?'

MacMurrough sighed a deep and long sigh of sorrow.

'Because there would then have been two of you dead instead of one,' he said. 'I could not stop him. He wrenched away from me, the plucky, foolish little fellow. I could have told him if only I had known ... O'Rourke's men are like himself, half savage. They likely thought the two of you were my own. How will I face his father?'

Richard was carried like a hero from the battlefield on a stretcher made of boughs, the first in the great funeral procession which returned to Ferns. Eighty-one of MacMurrough's treacherously slain men were buried in a huge mound outside Ferns, after three days of mourning. As they were laid to rest, their praises were sung in a special poem of grief and farewell composed by Mac-Murrough's chief bard, MacCriffan. Richard was taken to Glascarraig with the full honours due to a soldier and placed on a ship bound for Pembroke and home. After the monks had chanted the office of the dead, the Abbot of Glascarraig, in a great speech, bade him farewell with a final salute.

'Hail and farewell to Richard, youngest son of the Rightful Earl of Pembroke and Striguil! You were a lion in battle even though you were only a boy! You were the battle prop of the island of destiny and of the island of Britain as well! Fare you well! Go in God's own keeping!'

The ceremonies were so beautiful and the last speech

59

so glorious that Gwynn almost wished that it was he himself who had been killed so that the same words would have been said over him.

More sadness came to MacMurrough to prod him into new rage and more desire for vengeance. As he and his men licked their wounds, Fitpatrick, King of Ossory, sent his eldest son, Enna, home to him, blinded. Fitzpatrick had not been fooled. A spy had brought him the story of the strange men who spoke a foreign language training in secret. The Fleming Fitzpatrick's men had captured had proved the report right. Enna, a hostage for his father's good behaviour, had to pay the price. By Irish law, he could never become king with such an injury. Conor MacMurrough, now Gwynn's best friend, became the son of greatest promise.

MacMurrough fumed up and down his castle battlements, backwards and forwards, like a caged tiger.

'Where the living hell is Strongbow? Where is he, before we are all betrayed once more?'

The halls echoed to his temper and everybody except Gwynn and Wuff stayed out of his way.

'Everybody in Pembroke knows that Strongbow is afraid of bad luck,' said Gwynn to MacMurrough. 'Maybe he thinks Richard's death was a curse. If you ask me, he won't come unless we can prod him once more.'

'What can I prod him with now?' bellowed MacMurrough in despair.

'If I were the King,' said Gwynn importantly, 'I would order the monk who is the best painter in the abbey to paint a beautiful picture of Aoife and I would get the man who is best at talking, beside yourself, like O'Regan, to take the picture over to Strongbow right away.'

Dermot the King suddenly came to life.

'Gwynn,' he whispered. 'Go down at once to the abbey and say that the King orders the presence of Father Finbarr here in this castle.' His voice rose. 'Tell them he is not to come here without his quill and brushes. Tell them further that he is to come here even if he is on his death-bed.' MacMurrough's voice rose to a happy and excited shout. 'And tell them that if he is not here within half an hour, I will *put* him on his death-bed! Go!'

It was the first week of May 1169 when up the dusty road to Ferns from the south galloped MacMurrough's son, Conor, driving his horse to a foam of white sweat. In through the look-out posts, past the houses, streaked with dust and perspiration, on, on, on, until he had gained the gates of his father's castle. Seeing him on the battlements, Conor shouted in a frenzy of excitement, 'MacMurrough, my father, they are here! The soldiers from Wales have come!'

What a sight Conor MacMurrough reported! In Ireland a soldier wore ordinary clothes which blended with the countryside, but the Normans loved glitter and shine, colours and flags. Conor described them excitedly to his father and all his chief advisers. 'The first contingent has come — only the first — and what a thrill! Over five hundred men dressed like angels. White tunics with a big red cross on them over shiny armour flashing in the sun. They have helmets that cover the skull and nose, flags and shields and everything and each knight has his own emblem....' Conor paused to draw breath.

'Go on, go on,' his father urged.

'They have horse soldiers and foot soldiers, long bows and arrows, lances longer than a horse's body, horses with gear and medals jangling like bells, and they jabber away in all the languages — Welsh, Flemish and French.'

'Strongbow, boy, Strongbow?' his father demanded.,

'Strongbow will be here in a few weeks. The chief of the men who landed at Bannow Bay is called Fitz-Stephen. Father, he is so fast and determined! They are camped out, just waiting for your orders!'

MacMurrough jumped for his battle gear and sword. Orders swept around with gale force and women scarcely found time to say good-bye to a son or husband. Soon Conor MacMurrough and five hundred men were streaming south to meet the hired men who had landed.

MacMurrough, about to mount a prancing horse, yelled out, 'Come on, Gwynn, we are up off our knees.'

Then the King of Uí Chinsealaigh suddenly paused and pulled his horse to a halt. He looked down at Gwynn: 'You are too valuable to me to walk until you wear your legs out to the knees. Come here! I have a little present for you.'

Dismounting, he brought Gwynn across the yard to the stables and signalled to the stable hands. In a second they led out a beautiful jet-black pony with a white star between bright big eyes.

'He's yours, Gwynn. His name is Mish. That's short for *misneac*, the Irish for bravery. He is trained so well that he can sing songs.' MacMurrough laughed.

Gwynn was beside himself with joy, unable to thank MacMurrough because he could not think of words to say. Nor was there time. Already the main body of Uí Chinsealaigh's fighting men were on the march, well on the way and MacMurrough was now off after them in the rearguard.

Gwynn jumped up on to his pony. Mish gave a little prance for fun, Wuff danced around barking, and off they trotted to join MacMurrough. At last Gwynn had a horse of his very own and was no longer a passenger.

By the time MacMurrough had completed his triumphant march to Bannow Bay, many of his old friends and chieftains, who had feared for their lives while he was in eclipse, came out of hiding to join him.

Then as he stepped forward to meet the Normans, he was greeted by O'Regan.

O'Regan had played his part well. Strongbow had melted before the beauty of the girl in Father Finbarr's painting and the rest was easy. He had sent first-class men of battle experience. MacMurrough was introduced to FitzStephen, whom he greeted with a bear hug and a back slap. He inspected the men, discussed plans, targets and tactics. Gwynn moved excitedly amongst the Welsh soldiers and heard all the latest news from Wales and his family. The two armies stayed there by the lapping waters of Bannow Bay and spoke long into the night by the camp fires.

That night MacMurrough decided on the first target for attack — the Viking stronghold of Wexford. It was a mortal danger to have at his rear. It was owned by men who had deserted him, and its capture would mean wages for his hired soldiers. What was more, it was a safe port through which more men could come.

At dawn the next day, the augmented battalions of Uí Chinsealaigh were up like stirred wasps. Horns and drums sounded. MacMurrough's huge voice roared out but one word and made it sound like a thunder clap.

'WEXFORD!'

There was a wave of cheering and the multi-coloured lines of men, horses and baggage moved off from the shore.

There would have been less cheering had any of them seen the four Viking helmets over four pairs of wondering Viking eyes spying on them from the sand dunes the previous day. Even as the march on Wexford began, the Norsemen, well warned and fortified, were preparing a hot welcome for MacMurrough.

# 5   By Fire and Water

The Wexford Vikings were able to gather an army of two thousand fighting Norsemen. With smiles on their lips and murder in their hearts they marched far out of Wexford to wipe out MacMurrough. What were their feelings now for him? Once he was their King, who brought them good fortune and trade. He was now, they thought, a bluffing, toothless, half-dead wolf, but like all dying beasts dangerous.

A shock faced the Norsemen as they scrambled to the slopes of Forth mountain outside the town. All around MacMurrough's brown-clad marching men they saw a new army that glittered in the sun. There were four or more different sorts of soldiers. There were archers, horsemen with lances, swordsmen with coloured shields, horse-drawn wagons of supplies, food, the whole force in charge of section commanders. The Vikings turned and fled back to the walls of Wexford as fast as their legs could carry them.

The local Irish of MacMurrough's race lived outside the walls of Wexford, in communities clustered around little churches at Selskar and the Faythe. The Norse chief of Wexford, Thorkild, ordered every one of their houses burned to the ground, so that they could not give cover or shelter to any of MacMurrough's men. That done, they slammed and bolted the great gates of fort-ress Wexford and made ready for battle.

Gwynn had to force and coax Mish through the hot

ashes, while Wuff kept up a chorus of yelps. The cries and wails of the women and children who had been burned out rang in their ears. Some of the men had tried to fight back with sticks and stones. Their bodies smouldered with the ashes, as the breeze whipped up tufts of burning straw thatch.

'What are you going to do, MacMurrough?' asked Gwynn, as the tears streamed down his face from the smoke.

'Never you mind what *I* am going to do.' Mac-Murrough sounded angry. 'But do you know what I want *you* to do?'

'No! What?' demanded Gwynn, hoping he would be ordered to torture Vikings with boiling oil or burn their town to the ground.

'I want you to do NOTHING!' MacMurrough barked. He waved Gwynn's protest away without listening. 'Today your job is to learn,' he continued. 'I want you to look, to listen, to watch every plan and attack as it works — or does not work. Today you are in a school learning to be a commander of men in some great battle years ahead. Go where you want. Watch everything. But you are not to join in the fight and that is an order.'

Gwynn fumed and muttered crossly to Wuff and Mish. He was so enraged at the burning houses and the dead people lying around that he wanted to cut a Viking's head off and bring it home to his father for good luck.

The chief Norman commander, FitzStephen, stood with MacMurrough on the rocky hill of Carraigeen overlooking the centre of Wexford's strong walls. Between them and these walls was Wexford's wide graveyard. Gwynn watched as the Norsemen jeered and shouted catcalls from the walls. Soon they hoisted on poles a dozen severed heads and skulls of previous attackers and kept pointing to them. Gwynn gulped hard as a Norseman in full view smashed one of the heads to bits with a sword, as much as to warn MacMurrough's men that the same would soon comb their own hair.

'MacMurrough, we are ready,' said FitzStephen.

MacMurrough nodded and the old gleam of battle returned to his eyes.

'I will not wish you good luck, FitzStephen,' he said. 'I will only say this; if we take the town, the town is yours ... the quicker the better. Strike!'

FitzStephen roared an order in French and his men burst into activity, like ants. Some ran for the walls and covered their heads with shields so that all the shields together looked like a roof. Sheets of arrows whizzed through the sky on top of the Vikings and the clank of them hitting off wall and stone could be heard miles away. Then with bloodthirsty yells the Normans threw their scaling ladders up against the walls, six of them, all at the one time. In each case, a Norman soldier raced up the ladder, followed by half a dozen more. The Vikings waited until the first Norman was just at the top and then let him have a bucket of boiling oil right into his face and another bucketful for the men on the ladders underneath him. The screams of the scalded Normans were terrifying.

In three hundred and fifty years Viking Wexford had never been captured by storm, and for the rest of that day, the Norsemen, terrified themselves of MacMurrough's revenge, threw back every attack with gusto. They fought for their town like crimson devils.

They fired from the walls a hailstone storm of rocks, beams, bolts, ship spikes and boiling oil. Soon they were firing back the very Norman arrows fired against them, and all the while they kept up a rat-a-tat-tat din of noise by beating tin tubs. By dusk, FitzStephen and his Norman siege experts had had enough and they quit the walls to rest behind Carraigeen for the night.

The next day was the same, an exact copy of the previous day.

'Blast my soul and eyes, Gwynn,' MacMurrough shuddered during a lull, 'my own men would be just as good. This job might require brains yet, and not brawn. Be ready for action!'

On the morning of the third day of the attack, with the numbers of the dead and wounded rising, Wexford's Viking leader, Thorkild, came to the centre of the battlements. His yelling men fell silent and Gwynn winced as he heard him bawl an insult he knew was like a dagger trust to Dermot MacMurrough's heart.

'MacMurrough! Do you hear me?' Thorkild cried while he waved one of the withered heads dangling from a pole. 'Tomorrow, MacMurrough, we will bury YOU, with a dog, just like your rotten father!'

A wave of jeers and booing followed from the Viking walls before another hail of arrows and sling shots made their faces scarce.

'Tomorrow *you* will be dead!' shrieked back Gwynn and Wuff danced a jig with rage, but MacMurrough made no reply. His brow became creased the more he thought. Things were not going right. By now he should have been dining on venison in Wexford's Tholsel, using Thorkild as a footstool. He spoke at Gwynn without speaking to him, as if it were Gwynn who gave him his secret answers, just like the spirit of an ancestor.

'Thorkild came to the wall himself,' he mused. 'Then he said he would bury me with a dog *tomorrow*. Why *tomorrow*, boy? Answer me that ... why tomorrow? I will tell you, my boy. Thorkild knows that by tomorrow they will have help, more help from other Viking bases ... the Hebrides, Man, Shetland, Dublin. We have used up all our time. Follow me!'

MacMurrough went to the highest rock on Carraigeen, put his hands to his mouth and bellowed, 'Fitz-Stephen!'

The Norman chief looked up. MacMurrough gave the signal with upraised arms for a council of war. In five minutes the three main section commanders were before MacMurrough — FitzStephen, De la Roche, and Rhys of Wales.

From Carraigeen they could see the deep pool of the port of Wexford and the wide expanse of Wexford Harbour way out to the open sea. To the Vikings, it was safer, faster and far better known than dry land. Their ships, over forty of them, heaved gently with the tide's swell, ship against ship. Ships were easily the most important thing in the Viking world. Without them, the Vikings could never have flung themselves across the

world as they did, from America to the Black Sea. Wexford Harbour was packed with the best ships that the brains and skill of the Norse could make. There were long slim war vessels and broad-beamed ocean goers. There were richly carved pleasure vessels, and smaller trading vessels built for the Baltic and Irish Sea or coast where the waves were not as big as in the North Sea.

'We have one afternoon to take Wexford,' MacMurrough growled, 'or you may all go home. Thorkild the fool has said so, although that cutthroat did not mean to. He said the word "tomorrow". That means he will have more ships, more supplies, more men tomorrow. So you have from now until nightfall to do the job you were hired to do.'

Looking down on the ships, FitzStephen's Norman instinct came to the surface, for the Normans themselves were of Viking origin: 'There is only one way to settle this quickly. We must scuttle their ships!'

'Impossible!' snorted MacMurrough. 'They would see a swarm of bees going aboard their ships, let alone a troop of soldiers.'

Gwynn could contain himself no longer. 'They wouldn't see me, MacMurrough,' he burst forth. 'Let me go.'

'Shut up, I'm busy,' MacMurrough barked.

'Please, please, MacMurrough, you said I could go and see everything. Let me just go and see what the ships are like. I won't go *near* the town walls at all!'

Wuff barked with angry defiance in support.

'All right, all right!' moaned MacMurrough. 'Anything for peace! But tie that blasted whelp up or he will ruin you if he sees a rat.'

With howls and whines Wuff was tied up alongside

Mish at Carraigeen and Gwynn moved off at the back of the rocks.

MacMurrough shouted after him, 'Don't go into danger, and don't get caught! If you *are* caught, you will be a prisoner in Iceland for the rest of your life, with one arm or leg! They cut an arm or leg off boys they capture!'

Gwynn slid from rock to rock towards Selskar, hiding so that no Viking from the walls could see him. As he moved towards the still smoking ruins he could hear Wuff yowl and howl. He wondered if the Vikings had spies or guards down amongst the Irish outside the walls, dressed in Irish clothes, keeping an eye on their ships.

He came down from the high ground while the din of battle continued, but Wuff had stopped howling.

'He's either asleep or killed,' fretted Gwynn.

The next thing that happened was a horrible noise. 'Hurroo! I have you!' an Irish voice screamed.

Two big hairy arms were thrown around him and a knife was put to his throat. He tried to speak and it was well that he knew Irish, for when he blurted the name of MacMurrough the hairy arms let go. He looked up. It was an old man, half-mad, with his hair singed to the scalp and his clothes torn. Gwynn jumped like a rabbit to a safe distance from him and then told him in Irish that he was going to play in the boats.

'Play in the boats?' the old man bleated. 'You'll play then on your own.' He gave a mad shout and shuffled off, crying all the time, 'You'll play then on your own!'

Gwynn ran as hard as he could to get away from the fright and the poor man with the knife. Soon he was crunching through what was left of Selskar's houses.

Even after two days, beams of timber were still smouldering, and large heaps of red-hot ash were still smoking. Some women and old men were trying to clean up but most of them were just sitting there, looking at the lapping waters of Wexford Harbour, unable to think or work.

Gwynn wished he had Wuff for company, and the wish had hardly entered his head when there was a wild scampering. The same Wuff jumped up into his arms, licking him and barking, while the chewed-off rope still tied around his neck wagged like an extra tail. Delighted, Gwynn set off on the most urgent part of his important mission, warning Wuff to keep quiet.

There was a causeway, just like a pier, running from Selskar Church down to the rock just off the shore where the ferry crossed. It gave a full view of the waterfront and was lined with hide-bound currachs and fishing smacks. Just below them to the south lay the fearsome looking Viking fleet with gaping curved figure-heads and furled sails, all rising with timbers bumping, groaning gently with the heave of the tide. Their heavily tarred timbers and hide-bound parts, sails and riggings, hot in the sun, were parched by an east wind blowing into the town.

To Gwynn's great astonishment, not a single sailor stood on guard. The Vikings evidently thought it unnecessary, as the ships could be seen from the town walls. For a while he pretended to play around the boats, just in case anyone was looking. But sooner or later he intended to try and inspect the Viking ships themselves. He was well used to the waters and boats of Pembroke so he pushed out a light Irish currach and Wuff and he jumped on board. With a single light oar, he let the currach drift south with the flowing River Slaney.

He reached the Viking fleet within minutes, bumping in under a trading vessel loaded with grain. It was no good for the plan Gwynn now had bubbling in his mind. He floated further on. The next vessel was empty, but the third ship was the very one he was looking for. If he had planned a ship to set the world on fire, this was it! There was not a man on board and the tents used by the crew were still standing. There were at least twenty-five bundles of feathers, yards and yards of sail-cloth and the timbers of the ship had been newly drenched in tar. Two other ships were wedged between it and the waterfront and they themselves were smack alongside every other vessel, all the way down to the packed deep pool of Wexford port. There were even more ships there than he remembered, so some more must have docked during the night.

Gwynn was neither challenged nor stopped; he might just as well have been a Viking boy fishing for crabs. Suddenly he was conscious that there was not a moment to lose. If he was to strike a blow for Dermot Mac-Murrough he could only do so while the wind blew from the east and while the tide was going out. It had to be done at once so that his currach could slip back quickly to the Viking ships — and he would have to do it on his own!

He was in a fever of excitement as he beached again at Selskar. His heart pounded at the thought that his plan might succeed, but he knew that if he was caught, even in the attempt, the Norsemen would burn him alive. He searched and soon found several earthen jars lying near the waterfront — wine, milk and butter jars, thick enough to withstand hardship on water. Some leather thongs would also be of use. He went to a house which still had burning timbers and red-hot ash, and with a hand shovel he had found nearby, he filled each of the four jars he had selected with a mixture of red-hot ash and smouldering timber pieces, quickly loaded them on to the currach and pushed off into the Slaney current. Inside one minute, his currach with the four smoking jars was skimming the waves towards Wexford's Viking fleet.

Then horror struck! A line of Viking ships had entered Wexford Harbour from the open sea, and although five miles away, the wind was in their sails. More help was arriving for the Norse garrison and Gwynn was trapped unless he worked like forked lightning. The fright lent demon strength to his limbs.

He gripped the thongs and hurled the lightest of the fiery jars into the middle of the cargo of feather bundles and sail-cloth. Then he fired a second jar. The feathers and cloth burst into flames, the very same as a furze bush fire, fanned by the east wind. Gwynn pushed on to the next ship, hurled the third jar close to the furled sails, and finally the last one into a third ship. The flames from one ship seemed to act as a magnet for the next ship. Soon they were all huge balls of fire. A sweep of flame crackled through the air, giving its grim message to the Vikings of Wexford.

Horns blew and alarm bells struck from the town, and hoarse howls of rage and warning split the wind and waves. Too late! The packed vessels untouched by fire so far could not be rescued. They were moored to the waterfront and the outside vessels, now searing wind-swept furnaces, jammed them all in. Helplessly the Norsemen watched. None of them had ever dreamed of, or expected in any way, ever, danger from the very waters they were masters of.

Gwynn rowed back feeling twenty feet tall and the light currach flew half way up the beach at Selskar. The Irish whose houses had been ravished awoke, as if from the dead, to laugh, dance and cheer as their tormentors' ships burned. Gwynn was in no danger now, for the black smoke was blinding the Vikings inside Wexford's walls.

Now there was another twist to the saga. The Viking ships which had just entered the harbour, terrified by the blizzard of flame, sparks and smoke, turned about and headed for the open sea while the outgoing tide still gave them a chance. With Wuff yowling behind him, Gwynn gained the height of Carraigeen where Mac-Murrough was directing operations. Already the black smoke with the stench of burning hides reached up into the sky. The attacks on the walls had stopped and the battering ram crews were gathering on the green rocky verge to watch the town catch fire.

Gwynn marched up to MacMurrough with glory in his voice and a proud boast that could not be contradicted.

'MacMurrough,' he announced, 'your trouble here is over! I have set Wexford on fire!'

All the words that the big frame of MacMurrough could utter were, 'I don't believe it! I don't believe it! I don't believe it!'

It wasn't long until he did believe it. Within half an hour, with flames licking their backs, the Wexford Vikings decided that they did not want to end up as lumps of charcoal. All the great gates opened and out poured the whole Viking population — garrison, men, women, children, animals — all blinded with smoke and soot, coughing, vomiting, falling on the ground, not caring and not sure whether they were alive or dead. Among them was the figure of their rash chief, Thorkild, begging for mercy. MacMurrough showed some mercy, but not too much.

'I will not bury you as you were to bury me — with a dog. I will put you where you belong, where the people you made suffer can see what you are. I will put you on show like a dog, with a dog.'

That night, MacMurrough's carpenters made a stout cage of timber creels and fixed it up on a horse's cart. All night long, the cowering Thorkild was taken in it around the outskirts of Wexford town from Selskar to the Faythe, forward, back and through the smokey streets. It took superhuman strength on the part of Mac-Murrough's men to keep hundreds of screaming women from tearing him apart. In the cage with Thorkild, Mac-Murrough placed a diseased, scurvy, mongrel dog.

Gwynn was a hero. When the story of his marvellous feat spread, he rode nowhere around Wexford on Mish without cheers in his ears. MacMurrough was very proud of him because, after all, he had discovered him in the first place. The people around the town took heart again so great was the victory, and they started to clean up the rubble. The Vikings were put to work to make Wexford's defences as good as before and to make the port first-class for either war or peace, trade, fishing or pleasure.

MacMurrough himself grew from strength to strength. He decided not to put any Viking soldier to death, not even Thorkild. They were too useful as fighters. He brought them together and told them they would not be beheaded provided, and only provided, they swore a final and lasting oath of allegiance and obedience to him. This they agreed to do willingly. More than that, they agreed to join MacMurrough's army and fight wherever he directed them. Thorkild was released from his cage and fought like a badger ever after for MacMurrough until the day he fell in battle.

Back in Ferns with his spoils, MacMurrough mused on what he might yet do — if he had more help. But storm clouds were gathering ahead. Rory O'Connor, High King of Ireland, could no longer disregard the success at Wexford. MacMurrough would have to be put down, and so a great army was gathered to march on Uí Chinsealaigh.

Forewarned, MacMurrough prepared his battlefield, the jungle between Ferns and the mountains known as *Dubhtir,* the black country, a dark gloomy place of closed foliage, a booby trap of marshes, streams and thickets. Trees were felled, the underwood plashed, the surface of the level ground turned up by digging deep pits and trenches, and numerous secret and narrow passages cut through the thick undergrowth and trees. Into this maze of traps, he packed his men.

The army Rory O'Connor had assembled to overwhelm MacMurrough included two of his bitterest enemies, Tiernan O'Rourke and Dermot O Maoil Seachlainn of Meath, and the Norsemen of Dublin. They all believed MacMurrough had not a leg to stand on — FitzStephen's squadron was dismissed as 'not worth notice'. But, confronted with that grim dark battlefield, Rory O'Connor drew back; he would try to negotiate fair terms instead.

Gwynn, in the vanguard of Dermot's alert army, blinking behind the cover of bushes and briars, watched as the two greatest military commanders in Ireland met. He heard the usual shouted introductions by their right-hand men, saw them dismount and walk towards each other, but he could not make out the conversation between the two kings. At first there were shoulder shrugs between them and then arm gestures, as if each man was saying, 'the way it looks to me is like this'. They walked up and down, occasionally stopping to emphazize something with jabbing fingers. The only important pointer was that no voice was raised in rage.

After a full hour of exchanges, head shakes as well as nods, smiles and frowns, the two most powerful monarchs in the land slapped each other's right hand. A deal, whatever it was, had been struck, and a witnessed hand slap in Ireland meant a bargain. O'Connor withdrew to the head of his column, turned to face the Mac-Murrough lines and waited.

MacMurrough walked his horse slowly back to his men, a frown upon his face. He then brought his finger up to his lips to order silence, Then, as was his habit, the furrowed frown turned to beaming grin and his ranks had to fight to choke their cheers. When he got abreast of his commanders and Gwynn, he stopped.

'Gentlemen, we have an agreement! But NO NOISE!' he warned with a raised voice. Silence was maintained. Then he called Gwynn and Conor:

'Come here to me, the two of you.'

Conor MacMurrough and Gwynn jogged smartly across to him.

'Conor,' said MacMurrough, 'I have very good news

for you! You're about to take part in a big adventure! The PRESENT High King of Ireland,' MacMurrough chuckled, 'has offered to recognize me as King of Leinster and the Norsemen, provided I send the hired help back. Of course I told him I had only a fistful, a useless lazy crowd of bores eating our food. That was a good stroke all right — he thought there were thousands!

'So he next offered to recognize me in all my former titles — even some I had forgotten — provided I recognized him as King of All Ireland. Now for the time being there's nothing wrong with that, so I said, "Certainly, O'Connor". He became as gay as a thrush on a dead cat's back.

'He now invites *you*, Conor, to go back to Connaught with him, not only as a hostage for my good behaviour but for something of much greater importance altogether. He wants to arrange a happy marriage between you and his little girl. Isn't that lovely? Isn't that the best one you've ever heard?'

'All right then,' replied Conor, 'but I'd like to see his little girl first. She might be awful! And what about me ... if you make a move against him again?'

MacMurrough's grin froze to a look of violent determination.

'He would not have the spleen to cut your fingernails. Because of one thing he is sure; I would waste Connaught and cut down every O'Connor to the last half loon ... and don't you forget that, my boy, *for one minute,* even if your head is under the water for the third time. Now, get to hell up there, and remember you are a MacMurrough in the O'Connor nest. But trust no one! Not even that lovely little girl. Go now!'

Conor, dazed at the sudden turn of events, had hardly

time to think about a long good-bye.

'I'll see you soon, Gwynn, and I'll tell you everything.'

A rough, fierce embrace from his father and he was gone, soon smothered in the O'Connor ranks, which turned west for the mountains.

As they watched the departing army, MacMurrough, O'Regan and FitzStephen gathered in a huddle.

'You know why he wants my boy?' asked MacMurrough. Then he answered his own question: 'He wants him because as HIS son-in-law I would not move against him. That means only one thing; Rory O'Connor realizes that I am the greatest, and only, threat to him in Ireland today!'

It was possible, even for Gwynn, to see the fever grow in MacMurrough from that moment. Time was all important, as the dream of a MacMurrough monarchy ruling all Ireland forever in security fanned Dermot's imagination.

In the meantime, good luck smiled upon him. A further small contingent of first-class mercenary veterans landed at Wexford to join him. This totalled ten knights, thirty mounted cavalry men and a hundred archer marksmen under FitzStephen's half-brother, Maurice Fitzgerald. MacMurrough dispatched Fitz-Stephen over to the Atlantic coast of Munster; when he returned, he had an alliance for MacMurrough with the most influential ruler in the south-west of Ireland, Donal O'Brien.

The next stop was to consolidate his power in Leinster. MacMurrough in a hurry became a ruthless Mac-Murrough, and the new tricks of war, learned by the

Normans from the battlefields of Europe to the burning deserts of Asia Minor, swept aside all serious opposition. And as the spring of 1170 advanced, Dublin, the greatest Norse city outside Scandanavia, fell to him like a rotten apple from a tree, without the loss of a man. MacMurrough set fire to every house in the suburbs around Dublin, and the sparking smoke-belching inferno looked like the end of the world to the defenders behind the walls. The Norse ruler Asculf submitted without battle, recognizing MacMurrough as overlord. He, too, was buying time. Nevertheless, to Ireland and the nearby world, Dermot MacMurrough was, beyond question, King of Leinster and the Norseman once more.

If all that could be gained at such small cost, what could he not do with an army of bankrupt fanatics?

With the wind of victory at his back, the war fever gripped MacMurrough. There was no time to lose and little time to rest. But his great plans needed reinforcements from Wales — and where the living hell was Strongbow? If he did not arrive soon, the whole thrust of the campaign would be lost. He must come now.

MacMurrough ordered emissaries at once to Wales: 'Dermot, son of Murrough, King of Leinster, to Richard, Earl of Striguil, son of Earl Gilbert, sends greetings. Neither winds from the east nor the west have brought us your much desired and long expected presence. Let your instant activity make up for this delay and prove by your deeds that you have not forgotten your engagements but only deferred their performance. The whole of Leinster has already been recovered, and if you come in time with a strong force, the other four parts of Ireland will be easily united to the fifth....'

# 6 Strongbow Arrives

On the south coast of Wexford there is a peninsula which stabs into the Atlantic ocean. On the west side is Waterford Harbour, with a water route into the heart of Munster. On the eastern side, Bannow Bay knifes into Dermot's kingdom.

From remote prehistory, the peril of those two sea highways was recognized. On the Waterford side there was a heavily defended fort called Dun Cannon, Dun being the Irish for fort; while on the Bannow Bay side there was a deeply banked and defended little peninsula called Dun Donnell. The choice gave MacMurrough the option of striking at either Waterford or Wexford. But it was no longer in friendly hands; the local chieftain MacBrain had repudiated MacMurrough when the King was on his knees. Accordingly MacMurrough ordered, from Wales, a force to capture and reinforce Dun Donnell.

Meanwhile he fumed helplessly at home in Ferns. Even Gwynn was afraid to go near him, as he paced up and down, up and down. There was plenty of news and promises but no action.

Then on May day, an exhausted rider, one of the five men sent by Dermot to Dun Donnell to assist in the expected Norman landing, galloped up to the gates of Ferns Castle. Gwynn and the entire staff of the castle, chiefs, bards, clergy, with all the women, raced at speed to the great ground hall to hear the news, good or bad.

But there was little good news; it was all bad!

No great army had arrived. No fleet of ships. No victory-hungry soldiers. No Strongbow. Only one miserly ship had landed at Dun Donnell. It was commanded by Raymond, nicknamed 'le Gros' (the fat), and he had with him only ten knights and seventy archers.

'The curse of Patrick and Columkille and Brigid and Moling on the useless hounds of hell,' roared MacMurrough. 'Are they still there? And where are the rest of *your* group?'

Then came the news that struck terror into the hearts of all the hearers.

'MacMurrough, listen to me. My comrades are dead. Slaughtered by the Waterford Vikings. They found out that Dun Donnell was fortified and in our hands. They sent an enormous army to wipe out le Gros and his men. Le Gros saw them coming and ordered us out to attack first, but even though his archers killed them by the dozen, they kept coming at us. Finally, we ran pell-mell back behind the earthworks. There was only one gateway through the defences and the Waterford men raced through. It was like a crowd struggling to get out of a church door on Sunday. The Normans started to pick them off in dozens. Soon it was a massacre. They kept coming through, thinking, I suppose, that their Vikings were wiping out the Normans, but it was they who were being slaughtered. Out of about three thousand, seventy were left alive and, MacMurrough, it was discovered that most of them were Waterford merchants, worth the ransom of the city.'

MacMurrough cheered up.

'Hell's fire, man, that's a good job anyhow. So we will

walk into Waterford without a scratch! By hell, we might make Gwynn here the Chief Magistrate, eh, Gwynn, how about that?'

He laughed at the thought but soon his laugh was wiped out. His messenger twitched with fright and memory.

'No, we won't, MacMurrough! Raymond le Gros has an adviser from Wexford called Harvey. This lunatic told le Gros that unless the fright of Satan was put into the Vikings' hearts to freeze them for ever with fear, it would be better to go back to Wales and starve.'

Gwynn now knew that something terrible beyond the thinking of man had taken place. MacMurrough, even after a lifetime of battle, sensed the same. Almost in a hush, he asked, 'What did they do?'

His messenger had difficulty with the reply.

'They first of all threw the wounded over into the sea. But the seventy who were alive and well, the rich merchants, they took them, and one by one, they broke their legs and then fired them alive into the Atlantic from the cliff tops, and it didn't matter how much gold they offered or how loud their screams for mercy. Mac-Murrough, the land of Erin is a sword land, it is true from ancient times, but after that deed the heavens themselves grew dark and a terrible black storm lashed the fort. I left with my stomach sick, not caring what end became of me or them. MacMurrough, they have brought a curse on us. I feel it in my belly!'

Gwynn shuddered with the shock but MacMurrough did not speak for several minutes. He stayed as if paralyzed, on the one stone flag. What had happened had been done, and would be seen to be done, in his own name and authority. Then, he gave his verdict.

'We will leave them there to starve and rot. Let time and enemies plague them. If they survive well and good. I will see to it that a pleasant rest in a grave, even the Atlantic, will be easier than the load I'll put on their backs. The rest of you get yourselves trained. That means you too, Gwynn. You're a child no longer. I want men as fast as greyhounds and as hard as oak when Strongbow lands. For better or worse, we have cannibals fighting alongside us now.'

On 23 August, 1170, Strongbow disembarked at Passage, near the place where the Suir, the Nore and the Barrow rivers meet in Waterford Harbour. With him were two hundred Norman knights and a thousand other heavily armed soldiers of fortune, soldiers who would fight anywhere, for anyone, as long as the wages were good. He marched towards Waterford's walls, with the fear and determination of the trapped in his heart. His king, Henry the Second, had learned of his plan to go to Ireland, and fearing that he might start a rival kingdom at his back door had ordered an instant halt to the whole adventure, an order that if disobeyed would cost Strongbow his life, lands and fortune. But Strongbow held firm. He sought out two wealthy Jewish money-lenders in York city, and they loaned him the money to arm his men to the teeth and shipped them to Ireland. Now he had no other future except to fight like a lion, conquer and gain wealth in Ireland or die in battle — or be hanged. He hoped MacMurrough would never find this out; if he did it was not Aoife or her promised kingdom of Leinster that would keep Strongbow company. It would be the strands of a rope around his neck.

Meanwhile, there was Waterford to look forward to, and that would be a tough nut to crack. It was shaped like a fortified triangle, with massive steep walls and a huge round tower at each of its three corners, bounded by water on two sides.

In Ferns time hung heavily on everyone's hands. Mac-Murrough waited hourly for news from Strongbow at Waterford. Gwynn, missing Conor more than he could have imagined, wandered around aimlessly. Aoife, whose future would be decided by what was happening thirty miles away, was moody and abstracted. She and Gwynn talked endlessly of what the future might bring.

'But they'll never take Waterford,' she told him. 'Didn't they tell you about the giant?'

'Giant,' said Gwynn, 'what giant?'

'My father must have told you about the giant. Every fool knows about the giant! I want to know what he said about him.'

'Your father said nothing to me about any giant and he tells me everything,' Gwynn replied crossly, as Wuff growled. 'You're making it up.'

'Well, of course,' said Aoife, 'if you want to know nothing about him, I don't mind. But wait until you see him tear men in two. As for you, he would eat you and that dog in one swallow, that's all!'

Gwynn was about to change the subject; then he had second thoughts. If there really was a giant, then the more he knew about him the better.

'All right then, tell me about your famous giant,' he said, thinking to himself he would only believe it after he had actually seen the giant tear two, three or even four men in two.

'If you don't believe me, ask any of the men,' said Aoife with an airy wave. 'I don't care. You'll know soon enough. He's the Viking's secret weapon in Waterford. They always bring him into battle when things go badly.'

'I thought he was an Irish giant,' snapped Gwynn, 'out of the forests.'

'He's not even Viking!' Aoife sounded mysterious.

Gwynn's curiosity was really aroused. Maybe he was half horse half man or something like that. He had heard stories of giants with men's bodies and boars' heads back in Wales, and hadn't there been an Irish king who was born under a curse, with the ears of an ass?

'Go on!' he shouted. 'What sort of a giant is he then?'

'He is the greatest, the most terrible and the most magical giant in the world,' Aoife declared. 'The Vikings captured him away beyond Iceland, beyond Greenland, in a land across the Atlantic ocean, even further away than the Land of the Fish, and that is at the end of the world. He is bigger and broader than the biggest bull you have ever seen and his skin is the colour of a horse's nose. He wears feathers in his hair in battle, and has colours painted in stripes across his face. He speaks queer noises. No one knows what he says, but his name is MoggWaw.'

'I never heard anything so ridiculous in my whole life,' scoffed Gwynn. 'If no one knows what he says, how do they know when he is hungry?'

Aoife remained calm.

'He does this,' she replied, pointing her finger to her open mouth and then to her stomach. 'The Vikings are very glad to feed him, too. He has won battles on his own. They only have to get him excited.'

'More lies,' thought Gwynn to himself, but he pretended to believe her. 'What does he do when he gets excited?' he asked.

'He goes around with a strange chant like hee, wow, wow, wow, hee, wow, wow, wow, and lets out a terrible scream every now and again. He chews with his fangs the man's heads he tears off.' Aoife made a munching sound. 'Five years ago a pirate ship tried to dock at Waterford and MoggWaw jumped from Reginald's Tower into it. He was so heavy that his legs went straight through the boat's timber planks. The boat sank and all the pirates drowned. MoggWaw only shook himself and walked up the strand, chawing one of the pirate's arms just as if it was a pig's crubeen. I'm sure at this moment he's crunching a Norman breastplate in his teeth. So, you see, that's why they'll never win at Waterford.

'Anyway,' her tone changed to petulance, 'I'm not sure I want to be married and tied to this Strongbow fellow. Everyone keeps telling me how marvellous he is ... I'm sure now he's a horror.'

Gwynn had nightmares all night and dreamt that the giant was dipping himself and Wuff in gravy and washing them both together down his throat with a cauldron full of ale. Next day, when he got a chance, he questioned MacMurrough.

'You never told me about the giant,' he said very crossly.

'Giant my backside!' MacMurrough shouted. 'You and your giant! If I was down there in Waterford, we'd have taken the city by now and I'd have that fellow in an iron net this very night, swinging by the heels out of Reginald's Tower.'

'Why aren't you there?' ventured Gwynn, almost afraid to ask the question.

'Wait and see ... wait and see ... that has to be the plan of the moment. Do you think I like being cooped up here while Strongbow is having all the action?'

'Talking of Strongbow,' said Gwynn, 'Aoife said she is sure he is a horror and that she might not marry him.'

MacMurrough let out a might roar.

'Is that so then? Well I'll tell you this. If Aoife doesn't make up her mind to marry Strongbow, I will make up her mind to marry MoggWaw, you wait and see!'

'That's terrible,' yelled Gwynn. 'You can't do that.'

'Women!' snorted MacMurrough. 'I don't understand them. If you praise someone, they don't like him. If you say he's a rotten blackguard they start to like him! Here I am, supposed to be in charge of a land and an army, rightly hoaxed up with women!'

'Well if so, you'd better blackguard Strongbow very hard, MacMurrough,' declared Gwynn, as wisely as a bishop.

The words were hardly out of his mouth when the gleam of a scheme crossed MacMurrough's face and he started to chuckle to himself.

'Send for Aoife,' he ordered.

When she came, he took her hands and spoke in a gentle caressing voice. 'I've changed my mind, child,' he said. 'About Strongbow and you.'

Aoife withdrew her hands abruptly.

'What?' she asked, like the crack of a whip.

'Well,' said MacMurrough, making a face, 'I don't like the looks of the rascal.'

'Oh!' said Aoife alertly, 'is it you who are going to marry him?'

MacMurrough continued as if she had not spoken: 'There's something now about the blackguard I don't like. He's mad for power. Everybody knows that. Do you know that that fellow has slit throats before now? He's a bad-tempered cur. I would not wish any father's daughter on him! And there's another thing — he's been around too much, all across the world. I declare to God he brought a rash of skin disease on him back from Jerusalem, and do you know what? There's still a smell off him. I wouldn't mind that in a way, if it wasn't for the mean way he pours his eyes over a body to see whether there's treachery afoot or not. I would not say now, child, that the fellow, with all I've done for him, even trusts you own poor father one little bit. No: You'd be ten times better off without him. Going into one of your father's convent foundations I think. You'd be spared the misery of a life with that leper anyhow.'

Aoife went silently white. Her lips tightened to a straight line and her eyes closed to slits as she thought of being in a convent for the rest of her life. Her voice went down to a whisper, but the words seemed to come out like a raking scream.

'I am to be taken to Waterford,' she declared icily, 'to meet Strongbow, the Earl of Pembroke.'

MacMurrough made a grimace, shrugged his shoulders and spoke several nothings.

'Well, well, that's the way of the world today! What am I to say! My ways are not your ways! Never a hill without a hollow, I suppose! Well, child, you'll have your wish. To Waterford we will go ... when we hear that the city has been taken. If it ever is! Maybe we should send Gwynn down, as our messenger, to find out what's happening....'

After an evening walking around the walls of Waterford looking for the easiest place to attack, Strongbow retired in a gloomy mood. The three-hundred-year-old Viking city state, which had never been taken by storm, would indeed be a tough nut to crack. There was no easy place to attack, but even if there had been the Vikings had decided to fight to the last man and the last house. They had heard about Wexford and the burnt boats. They had been shocked by the massacres at Dun Donnell. They were determined that wealthy Waterford would resist at all costs.

Next day, Strongbow hurled his men into action. With the sure command of a man who had seen battles and sieges won all across the western world, from the Sinai desert to the Atlantic ocean, he sent thirteen hundred men rushing at the massive stone walls of Waterford. Shouting, cheering, and under cover of a storm of swishing arrows, they fired their scaling ladders at the walls. It was just as in Wexford, except at the centre of the main wall. There Strongbow made his men put up three ladders together, alongside one another, to form one big ladder, so wide that three men were able to rush up it together, to the top of the wall.

But the attack was repulsed. The Normans re-grouped, and then threw themselves upon the walls of Waterford for the second time.

When Gwynn arrived, the attacking army had retreated and their leader was pondering tactics with Raymond le Gros, who resembled a starving skeleton. Brought before him, Gwynn announced himself a messenger from MacMurrough, and a Pembroke man as well.

'Come to see how we're getting on,' growled Strongbow in surprise. 'And where's MacMurrough? And his army? If you're the vanguard, you're the smallest one I've seen in my life. Well, stay around. I could do with another Pembroke man. With a bit of luck we'll have Waterford by Christmas.... Now, le Gros....'

Gwynn felt himself dismissed, something he had not been used to for months.

He set off for a walk alone, along the full length of the city's high walls, but well out of reach of sentries' arrows. Then, as he got closer to the waterfront where the walls ended at a strong round turret, he heard a strange noise, Strange for a siege, that is. It was the sound of a cross woman giving out. The voices were clear as a bell. The woman ranted on and on, while a man's voice grumbled occasionally in reply.

There was nobody in sight, so Gwynn wondered how he could possibly hear voices through the walls of Waterford, with ramparts at least thirty feet thick behind them. The moon came out from behind a cloud and suddenly the answer was before his eyes. The moon glinted on a tiny glass pane which had been very well hidden. That was it! A house had been built into the walls of Waterford! That meant only one thing — the wall at that point would only be as thick as a wicker basket, and the house itself would be an open door through the battlements.

Thrilled to fever pitch at his discovery, Gwynn crept back from the walls. As soon as he was sure no one had seen him, he took to his heels and raced to Strongbow's tent. He was tearing at the flaps when he was grabbed by guards.

'Strongbow! Strongbow!' he yelled at the top of his voice.

92

In an instant, Strongbow, buckling on belt and sword, was outside the tent.

'What's wrong, boy? What the hell is the trouble with you at this hour of the night?' he demanded. 'I'll take your sacred life if it's nothing important.'

'I know how to capture Waterford!' Gwynn blurted out.

Strongbow stared at him in disbelief. 'Go on,' he ordered.

'I have just found a way through the walls!'

Strongbow's voice crackled for le Gros and Fitz-Stephen. In a few seconds they were pacing in silence and speed down towards the River Suir's banks and the section of the wall where the house had been built. They dared not light lights to examine the wall but Strongbow's hands went over every inch of it within reach.

'Give me a dagger,' he whispered, and started to scrape and probe ever so carefully. Then he began to laugh softly. Gwynn was near enough to hear when he whispered to FitzStephen.

'The house is built into the wall like a bubble. It's disguised, but here's the best of it. Its only support on this side are two timber posts. They are there at the outside of the wall built into the ground — you can feel them for yourself! What would happen if we were to dig them away? Go and get me some good building men! And no noise! We will have to dig by the spoonful until daybreak.'

By dawn the plan was in order. The men had nibbled away slowly around the posts for hours. At sunrise the timbers were exposed and the soil around the butt of the posts was all scraped away. It was as if they just rested on the ground of an open field. Next, Strongbow had

93

FitzStephen collect a hundred of his best siege specialists. They slipped over one by one, and lay hiding under the wall near the house. A team of six horses was yoked to the two posts but the ropes were left slack, so that the horses appeared to be grazing.

At seven o'clock, Strongbow made a savage and deafening attack on the centre of the wall, far away from the doomed house, so that the Vikings would not see their real danger. At that moment whips cracked on the six horses. As they bolted, the ropes took the vicious strain. The posts supporting the house pulled out with a rumble and it collapsed in a roar of broken timber, masonry and dust. FitzStephen and his hungry hundred streamed over the ruins like locusts, followed by five hundred men, battle-axes, broad-swords, daggers, long bows and arrows in hand. They flooded the back streets, killing as they went, killing so fast that Viking bodies piled up in the streets and the blood ran like rivers. The defenders on the walls, caught on both sides, raced for the nearest round fortress. Instantly, the scaling ladders went up outside and the mixed horde of Norman, Flemish and Welsh catapulted over the walls like wolf packs after prey.

Sitric, the Viking chief, defended the last streets before making a final stand at Reginald's Tower. Shortly, it was all over and he was put to the sword in the spot he had so gallantly defended.

From the groans of devastated Waterford, Strongbow sent Gwynn back to Ferns to announce the capture of the city. MacMurrough's army of many colours bore down on Waterford, Aoife and Gwynn riding beside the King. When they arrived, just as at Striguil, MacMurrough and Strongbow dismounted and walked the last few paces towards each other, to embrace like brothers. Both armies cheered.

Aoife was then called forward. Trembling, she lowered her eyes to the ground although dying with curiosity. Secretly she was terrified of the awful scurvy she might see on Strongbow's face — that and the awful smell.

A voice broke the spell of silence. MacMurrough cleared his throat and made the blunt introduction that gave the information most important at the time:

'This is Aoife, the eldest daughter of my rightful wife, Mor, the grand-daughter of Donncha, the son of Murrough. This is Richard, Earl of Striguil, Rightful Earl of Pembroke, who is named Strongbow.'

Aoife shyly raised her eyes to his face. The man before her was fair of hair though it was tinged with grey. He was tall, honest-faced, in a helmet so bright and shiny that her face was reflected in it. His sword was strapped by a belt around a lean waist and his shin guards shone like silver in the sun. His hair and beard were trimmed so neatly that he looked like a statue on a bishop's tomb. Aoife was now smiling with relief and pleasure, and when Strongbow courteously bent from the waist to bow and say something in his soft French accent, the picture painted by her father of an evil-smelling blackguard was swept away for ever.

Four days after the capture of Waterford, Aoife, in white and gold, and Strongbow, in crusader's robes of red and white, were married by the Pope's envoy to Ireland, Giolla Criost, Bishop of Lismore. Waterford's Viking cathedral was used for the ceremony. Choirs sang, bells pealed, and the stone flags rang to the clank

of arms and suits of armour. Bishops with gleaming mitres marched beside visiting kings. And in that cathedral crowd some of the most important rulers in the south of Ireland, including the great King of Munster, O'Brien, had gathered. They could see that MacMurrough was back in power again.

After the wedding came the feasting. The vast Viking stores of wine, ale and food of all descriptions were drunk and eaten, to the sounds of singing, dancing and music, as more than a hundred harps strummed like an archangels' chorus.

By nightfall, when all was still again, MacMurrough sighed as he sat with Gwynn.

'You know,' he said, 'I have taken Waterford twice before now, over the years. But not by storm. I negotiated. No lives were lost.'

'Well, you saved the lives of Reginald the Viking and his Irish friend O'Faolain, just before they were to be cut down,' Gwynn reminded him.

'Still,' MacMurrough mused, 'too many were lost. We could have used them. But that's the way of the world ... that's the way of it.'

Just before a very tired Gwynn curled up and went to sleep he thought about Conor. How he would have enjoyed the excitement of the last few days! He wondered when he would see him again.

# 7 The Capture of Dublin

MacMurrough's great fist banged the oak table in Reginald's Tower, rattling the plates.

'Ireland is ours for the taking!' was his first sentence, and it was as good as a whole sermon.

It was time to be on the move again and he had summoned a great conference of war with all the leaders. Gwynn was present because he carried Mac-Murrough's maps and plans. The others who moved around the table were Strongbow, le Gros, Fitz-Stephen, De la Roche, and O'Regan.

'There is only one direction to take ... there is only one man in the way of our all-Ireland power,' said Mac-Murrough, who had become more feverish for action as his power base increased. With the string of fortresses and the firm allies he had mustered, from the Shannon river across to the Wicklow mountains and the Irish sea, it would be almost impossible for any other army to stop him now.

'... only one man in the way,' he repeated.

'Yes,' said Strongbow, 'Really there is only one man — O'Connor, the High King! We must take O'Connor!'

MacMurrough looked at his new son-in-law as if he had just sprouted five heads and a bushy tail. He was stunned to silence for a moment, then he croaked, 'O'Connor? That bloodless drink of water! Sacred blood, who said anything about that dandylion? All we have to do is appear to him and he'll go into a faint!

O'Rourke is the man! O'Rourke is the last malignant goat capable of putting spine into O'Connor! O'Rourke is the power behind O'Connor! O'Rourke has to be strangled first, *no matter what the cost*!'

MacMurrough almost smashed the solid oak with a pounding crash, as the passion of hate rose in him.

O'Regan broke the shivering silence. 'I think you have O'Rourke on your mind, like a phantom. O'Connor must be first. O'Rourke is nothing without O'Connor.'

'God help you,' growled Dermot. 'How do you think O'Rourke has survived the battles and struggles of the last forty years? Four decades since he first invaded us back in 1128? And now, with only swamps at his back, he stands to become High King — if O'Connor has a heart attack or the cholera! There's nothing in the eastern world to touch him for the talent of the beast, the treachery of the badger or the cruelty of the wolf.'

Gwynn's excitement rose at the thought of destroying O'Rourke, but for Strongbow there was a bigger prize.

'Very well,' he mused. 'We must march north in any event ... but why not take Dublin on the way? If we had three fortified armed cities, we could afford to wait in comfort and trap O'Rourke without any worry at all.'

'Too much to hope for,' said MacMurrough. 'O'Connor and O'Rourke are now awake. They know what we are about. They all know about your lunatics at Dun Donnell. Right now they must be preparing for battle. They will meet us to wipe us out, somewhere between here and Dublin. O'Rourke will see to that, and he will have every sword in the north and west of Ireland with him.

'I'll tell you something else. At this moment, the

Vikings of western Europe are flooding into Dublin to get revenge for Wexford and Waterford — even as we are talking here!'

Strongbow was deep in thought. Finally he spoke directly to his father-in-law: 'As Normans in Ireland, we are strangers in a strange land. Now we must make choice of one of two things: We can do what we have come to do without pity and subjugate our enemies by arms, or we set sail for home and leave this country to a vampire like O'Rourke ... I will march to Dublin with you, MacMurrough!'

'And I ... and I,' shouted FitzStephen and De la Roche together.

'Good!' said MacMurrough, 'but we must send some men a couple of days ahead of us to spy on their positions. We cannot afford one mistake, not *one* mistake! So far it is our enemies who have made the mistakes.'

'I'll go!' said Gwynn.

'No, you won't,' barked MacMurrough. 'It's a job for tough men.'

'So was Waterford's wall!' Gwynn yelled. 'Please let me go, MacMurrough! I might find another short-cut.'

MacMurrough thought for a while and then gave in. Gwynn was better than any man.

'All right, then!' he said, pretending to be cross, 'but take a good horse! Mish is too small and it's a two days' journey there and back. O'Regan, go with him, and take six of your best men from the Wicklow mountains with you. You know what to do.'

Then MacMurrough took O'Regan aside.

'You are to mind Gwynn better than your own self. Nothing must happen to him. Do you understand?'

'You can depend on me,' replied O'Regan.

Within half an hour, the party was galloping north toward the Wicklow mountains and the greatest Norse city outside Scandinavia, Dublin, Gwynn on a kind but very strong horse named Gelock, which meant moon.

The party on the spying mission stayed on the mountain ranges, passing by the beauty of Glendalough and then Glencree, on toward the slopes from where they could see Dublin and the shimmering sea spread out before them like a great map.

Then came the sight they had been afraid to think about. From the mountain slopes at Ticknock and Ballinteer, they could see a huge army assembling on the plain of Clondalkin, a little to the south-west of Dublin, toward which all the roads from the south converged. O'Connor, the High King, alarmed at MacMurrough's victorious campaign, and goaded by Tiernan O'Rourke, had ordered the greatest army ever assembled in Ireland to converge and occupy every road outside Dublin to the south. There they waited, poised by sheer weight of numbers to punish MacMurrough and hang his men and allies.

The spying party moved east toward the sea and that night crept close to Dublin's ramparts from the direction of the great monastery of All Hallows, founded by MacMurrough himself. Their worst fears were realized. Norse Dublin bristled with arms, men and ships; and there was no loophole for Gwynn to report this time.

There was nothing more to be done. The group on the spying mission slipped off silently southwards through Enniskerry, near the home of Dermot's queen. They crossed the Wicklow mountains and met Mac-Murrough's own great army at another of his abbeys, Baltinglass, on the River Slaney in the foothills of Wicklow. They had marched in great order and spirits from Waterford, leaving a garrison behind to keep it safe.

'It will be man for man this time, MacMurrough,' reported O'Regan. 'There will be two battles. One on the plain of Clondalkin, and *if* the day goes with us, Dublin after that.'

MacMurrough clenched his two fists on the hair of his head, as if to tear it out by the roots.

'Blast their rotting guts!' he cried. 'If only I could take them one at a time. As soon as we tackle O'Connor and O'Rourke, the Vikings will come out to cut us off and cut us down. Hell's curse to them, what will we do?'

Neither Strongbow, FitzStephen nor De la Roche could offer a solution. Certainly they could fight and fight well, but they did not know the country.

'They have set a trap at Clondalkin. They want you to walk into it, MacMurrough,' Gwynn said.

MacMurrough raised an eyebrow to the roof of his head. 'Then why should we go through Clondalkin at all?' he asked.

Strongbow shrugged with impatience, but Mac-Murrough continued, 'We can keep off the main roads. It's lovely weather for a mountain stroll! We could go through the mountains, out of sight, as far as Enniskerry and then slip across to the sea side at night. By daytime, we could be before Dublin, but O'Connor and O'Rourke would not see us at all! The city would be between them and us.'

Strongbow's eyes lit up at the idea.

'Yes! That's it! Take the Vikings from behind! Then we can get our revenge on O'Rourke!'

In two days time, one of the most extraordinary and

fateful events in all Irish history took place. As dawn rose on 21 September 1170, the Dublin Norsemen looked east from their strong walls to find an army, greater and more frightening than anything they had ever seen, ready for attack. MacMurrough, the monarch they had abandoned, was arraigned before them, flanked by three heavily armed contingents of Norman mercenaries, the most bloody fighters in the world. Their escape route to the open sea was cut off. The Norsemen and their aged ruler, Askulf, decided to negotiate another truce and asked for time to draw up an agreement with their one time overlord.

The gates were opened, the city was gained without a scratch, and the Vikings of that great citadel threw in their lot with MacMurrough once more. Soon the defiant black ravan battle standards were removed from the walls. Instead the MacMurrough arms flapped from every turret, with here and there a proud crusader's shield.

O'Connor and O'Rourke, at the head of their mighty horde, could scarcely believe what had happened. The greatest prize in western Europe was MacMurrough's. Without a contest! O'Rourke wanted action, but O'Connor had seen enough. He was not going to waste valuable men and time fighting for a Viking city's fortune when that city had betrayed his trust.

It was MacMurrough's turn now, after years of battle and hardship, to witness something just as incredible. O'Connor and his great army arose as one man and without so much as throwing a stone withdrew from their chosen battlefield before Dublin and Dermot MacMurrough! They withdrew to their far off kingdom of Connaught. O'Rourke, raving like a madman, went his own way, bitterly cursing, to Bréifne. Spies reported the route he had chosen.

MacMurrough lost no time. The wind was in his back with gale force. He whipped a force of men together, to follow and scourge O'Rourke. Gwynn joined him on the mission, while Strongbow brought up a rearguard, to be avenged for his son Richard. O'Rourke's wretched men were tormented and killed in small groups, Mac-Murrough contenting himself with overtaking and capturing eight or ten at a time. When the land of Bréifne was entered at last, not a single house, hovel, rath or dun escaped the wrath of MacMurrough and Strongbow.

As O'Rourke retreated the pillars of black smoke following him showed where his enemies were. Their hot breath was almost on his neck. Desertions started. His battered and scattered men vanished into the night and the forests. MacMurrough felt his blood lust rise. Finally he was about to corner the curse that had haunted him for forty years.

Day after day hopes rose and then were dashed. Finally, at the far extremity of O'Rourke territory on the slopes of Slieve Gory, MacMurrough was forced to accept defeat. The kingdom of Bréifne had been ravaged and wasted, but Tiernan O'Rourke had disappeared like the *shee gwee,* the Irish fairy wind that comes down like a whirlpool, sucking hay and corn stacks into the air before vanishing from sight.

# 8  O'Rourke's Revenge

Gwynn could see for himself a terrible change taking place in MacMurrough. As the King's map carrier, he was close enough to miss nothing. MacMurrough had only to bark, 'Liffey!' or 'Boyne!' and Gwynn would have the right river map under his nose. With Conor gone, MacMurrough came to depend more and more on Gwynn, but he forced a terrible pace, sometimes seeming not to notice that Gwynn was there at his side, busy as a bee. It was only at rough meals in field or castle that MacMurrough signalled how much he valued him.

'Give the boy enough to eat!' he always remembered to cry out. 'He will want it all!' followed, sometimes, by a wink at Gwynn.

MacMurrough worked like a driven plough horse who minds nothing but the open sod under his hoofs. Nothing else in the world mattered except his lifelong ambition — to become High King of all Ireland and to keep that rank and succession in MacMurrough hands. He seemed scarcely conscious of the family, friends and soldiers around him. He just drove himself and his men on and on, to the prize that lay before his grasp.

In the process, he forced the submission of the King of Meath, who was swept away by the lightning wave of MacMurrough's men. From that moment on, the title of Meath, the most precious and ancient in Ireland, was added in the great record book of his kingdom, *The Book of Leinster:*

'Dermot, the son of Donncha, the son of Murrough, King of Uí Chinsealaigh, King of Leinster, King of all Southern Ireland, King of Meath.' The last flimsy barrier to his great plan was O'Connor, the High King.

'All that is needed for his submission is an injection of real fright,' he growled to Gwynn.

'What about our hostage, Conor?' bawled Gwynn.

'Hostage my backside,' retorted MacMurrough, as if he thought Gwynn was a three-quarter loon. 'He wouldn't have the blasted guts. Anyhow, he wants him for his own girl.'

As the days grew short, MacMurrough lost the keen edge of his drive. But another man spent the winter in a fever of activity ... and his name was Tiernan O'Rourke. The beast had shaken the mud and blood of battle off himself. He was nursed back to health, cunning and hatred in secret. In the months of January and February, while MacMurrough mused over his last plan of war, O'Rourke saw and recognized Mac-Murrough's ice-cold strategy. He, MacMurrough, was ready, and *able*, to swallow all Ireland at one fast gulp. O'Connor of Connaught was only High King on paper, in the record books of Clonmacnois. A mixture of vengeance and terror seized O'Rourke to a greater extent than ever before. In mid-February he rounded up one hundred of his men and rode for Tuam where he presented himself to the High King. He laid before him, piece by piece, the awful truth. His reign, his name, his race and descendants, kingdom and power were finished, unless...

On the first day of March a delegation of Connaught officials waited on Dermot MacMurrough in Askulf's hall, Dublin. MacMurrough paid but little attention to

105

them until O'Regan read out the letter they bore. His weathered face flushed as the words rang out, but Gwynn's blood froze in his veins!

'You have broken the conditions of our Treaty of Peace. You have maintained and strengthened a host of foreigners in this island and yet as long as you remained inside the bounds of Leinster we bore it with patience. But now, regardless of your oaths to us and having no concern for the fate of the hostage you gave, you have broken the bounds agreed on and insolently crossed the bounds of your own territory. You will either restrain absolutely your men and your foreign bands or we will certainly have your son's head cut off and sent to you.' Signed, Rory the Great, O'Connor: High King of Ireland.

Gwynn said noting but grabbed MacMurrough by the arm in the desperate fear that they must have shared.

'He will kill Conor,' he hissed.

MacMurrough pressed Gwynn's arm in consolation and then released his grip.

'That little weed would not have the backbone,' he whispered. 'I would hang or blind all belonging to him ... men, women and children. The thing to do is to shock him into the senses. That's all that is wanted. A shock!'

He rose up from his seat and strode down to the spot where O'Regan stood with the Connaught parchment in his hand. He took it from O'Regan, and slowly tore it to pieces. Then he spilled the pieces on the ground, before the eyes of the Connaughtmen, stamping them into the damp flags.

'O'Regan, take this down,' he ordered: 'To Rory O'Connor, King of Connaught! Dermot, the son of

Donncha, the son of Murrough, King of Leinster and Southern Ireland and Meath, declares that he will not desist from the enterprise he has undertaken until he has reduced Connaught to subjection, a kingdom he claims as his own ancient inheritance, and until he has obtained with it the monarchy of the whole of Ireland.'

He turned to the Connaughtmen: 'Take that back to the dockleaf you have for a King, and be glad that you are left alive, and in *one piece*, to do so!' They fled Dublin.

Next day the shattered Rory O'Connor read the message and made ready for his last end. MacMurrough was right. As he had reckoned, he had just about frightened O'Connor to death. He had, however, made a fatal miscalcualtion. He had reckoned without one of the key figures in the drama, the man with the cancer of hate in his belly — Tiernan O'Rourke, whom he believed to be in hiding and half-dead.

When O'Rourke read MacMurrough's reply to O'Connor, his advice was blunt and instant: 'Cut the hostage down!'

Tiernan O'Rourke was the one man who really knew MacMurrough's weakness. O'Rourke knew that the one and only way to kill MacMurrough was to kill his son *outright* and the more savagely the better! The sight of Conor delivered dead in a sack, like a bullock for the market, would annihilate MacMurrough.

It was O'Rourke's finest hour. Defeated, with Bréifne in ruins and expecting final execution himself, he urged the executioner's axe for Conor MacMurrough. At first O'Connor refused. But Tiernan O'Rourke was made of sterner stuff; he knew the power and conquest game. His reply to Rory O'Connor laid the option on the line;

either the High King did as instructed, or it would mean
the end of the O'Connor dynasty as a royal ruling force
for ever.

He asked the Connaught monarch to join him in the
cathedral of Tuam. There, beneath the bejewelled relic
of the true Cross, O'Rourke placed his right hand on the
richly decorated book of the Gospels. He turned toward
O'Connor and spoke: 'I swear by God's Blood and
Sacred Wounds that neither you, nor yours, will remain
Kings in Connaught or All Ireland unless the hostage of
your one enemy, Dermot MacMurrough, who is fast
approaching, is put to death, at once.'

The gleam from his malevolent eye, in conjunction
with the glinting stained glass and sacred surrounds,
seemed to have a trance-like effect on Rory.

He knew that all O'Rourke had to do to finish
O'Connor ruling power was to walk away and leave him
to his lonely deserts. Cravenly, he capitulated. Conor
was doomed.

It was the first of April, 1171. A group of trotting horsemen approached the walls of Dublin. Remaining well outside the west wall and gate, they shouted at MacMurrough's sentry!

'Greetings to MacMurrough, the vermin, from Tiernan O'Rourke of Bréifne!'

Then they dropped a sack, turned tail and galloped away like racing horses.

The sack was brought to MacMurrough. Inside was the severed head of his son Conor, eyes open as in life but with an expression of terrible bitterness and anguish. Also in the sack was the medallion worn around their necks by all the royal MacMurroughs.

Gwynn put his hand to his mouth to stop his scream of pain. MacMurrough sat on the oak chair as if struck by a sledge-hammer.

As the word spread, ministers like O'Regan appeared, and soon Strongbow, FitzStephen and De la Roche bolted up the steps to the place where MacMurrough grieved. He did not speak a word to anyone; he just gripped the sack to his chest. An hour passed by. Two hours.

Then he began to rock himself back and forward, gently, keeping time. After another while he started to chant quietly to himself, keeping time with the rocking. He was chanting an old lament, handed down from generation to generation, known as a *caoin*. It is usually sung by a choir of women at the time of death, and to hear the hard gruff father sing it by himself, to himself, was almost unbearable. Gwynn held his hand and the old man gripped it tightly, softly keeping on with the chant. Then quite suddenly, after about three hours without stirring from the same position, he fell over on to the stone flags, oak chair and all, with a mighty crash, and was silent.

Dermot MacMurrough started to die. In a few days, he asked to be taken back to Ferns, even though it meant facing the grief and blame of a mother, sisters, a brother, and all those who loved Conor. From that time on nothing mattered any more. The son upon whom he had set so much store, the son of glittering royal future, was now a beheaded corpse, cut down by his own hand, as surely as if he himself had wielded the battle-axe.

Gwynn, choking with despair, rode alongside the horse-drawn stretcher as the King was returned to Ferns Castle. It was an eerie fortress now, the feelings of those there a mixture of grief and abuse, as well as pity for the dying Dermot MacMurrough. Every day Gwynn tended him and told him all the news — not that there was much, since all activity had stopped.

MacMurrough's speech came back but he was unable to talk except with one side of his face. Gwynn could see, too, that he had the use of only half his body, from his head to his right foot. He always turned away from Gwynn when he spoke and turned sideways on his couch. Sometimes he would murmur, 'O'Rourke', and start to tremble, then Gwynn would hold his hand again until the trembling stopped.

Early on the first day of May, Gwynn was woken up by O'Regan. He said simply, 'He is calling for you!'

Gwynn threw on his tunic and went into the King's chamber, where MacMurrough lay with his back to him. He was unable to move, but he could speak slowly.

'Gwynn, I *want* you to go home for a while to your mother and father. Promise me you will go!'

Gwynn nodded, although his heart was breaking.

'Good boy! Take Mish with you. There is something else. My son is dead. I want you to take his place. I would like you to be my foster son. It is a very old, very close Irish bond, but *you* have to agree to it. I cannot make you. It is hard too, because you have to be a *real* son of mine, brave and good, and you must promise, always, everywhere, to do your best, no matter what you are at.'

'Yes, I promise,' Gwynn blurted. 'I will be your son, and I will tell everybody the truth about you, always.'

MacMurrough sighed a deep sigh and nodded his head to O'Regan. O'Regan went toward MacMurrough and took an object from the King's hand. It was Conor MacMurrough's chain and medallion bearing the royal MacMurrough coat of arms. He placed it around Gwynn's neck and his eyes glistened.

'You must go home now, Gwynn, for a while,' whispered O'Regan. 'The King is going into a long deep sleep.'

Gwynn left the high towers of Ferns Castle on Mish, and with Wuff barking at his heels he headed towards Boolavogue and Glascarraig, a ship, Pembroke and home. As he trotted down the hill past the abbey gates, he stopped. He turned Mish around and looked back across the silent valley towards Ferns Castle. The drapes at the window of MacMurrough's chamber had been pulled back. Knowing that MacMurrough would hear him, he cupped his hands to his mouth and his shrill yell echoed off the walls of MacMurrough's chamber.

'MacMurrough! I will be coming back! I will be coming back, and I will hang Tiernan O'Rourke!'

111

# Author's Note to Teachers

The story of Gwynn's adventures with Dermot Mac-Murrough is a story; I hope a good story. In some places, I have deliberately simplified history, and the vast network of political and family contacts in Mac-Murrough's long public life (1126–1171), to avoid mental confusion. For example, three precious hostages were given to Rory O'Connor; I have used and emphasized but one, Dermot's son Conor.

For overseas readers, I should like to explain that Gaelic Ireland, somewhat like old Greece, enjoyed cultural, legal and linguistic unity, but political fragmentation. Each small kingdom was ruled by a king, in the proper definition of the word; those with ambitions each tried, in as much as it was in their power, to obtain overlord ruling power, firstly in any one of Ireland's five regions (*cuige,* translated today as province) and ultimately of all Ireland. The prime example of a politically skilful warrior king of a minor kingdom achieving unchallenged all-Ireland power is provided by Brian Boru, 'Emperor of the Irish', who was killed after his greatest victory at Clontarf in 1014.

*Suggested projects:* Norman remains in your town and neighbourhood; family histories; Norman influences on language, law, building, towns, family life; Church foundations of the Norman era; absorption of the Normans into Irish society. A really fascinating one would be the recreation of life in one of the early Norman castles.

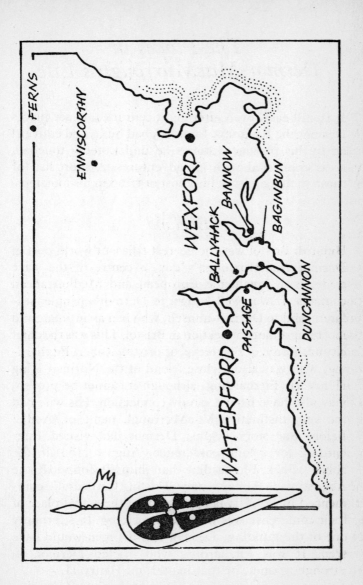

FERNS

ENNISCORTHY

WEXFORD

BALLYHACK

BANNOW

BAGINBUN

DUNCANNON

PASSAGE

WATERFORD

# The Places in Dermot MacMurrough's Life

It is still easy, even after eight centuries, to see places Dermot the King saw, founded, had built, and enlivened by his presence; stones he undoubtedly touched; areas connected with his adventures. A short list for those wishing to seek his ghost or tread in his footsteps.

## England

**Bristol:** Bristol was the nearest adjacent world port in Dermot MacMurrough's day, a centre of the slave trade, with invaluable European and Mediterranean contacts. It was well known to Dermot's people, seafarers, and to Dermot himself, who had an intimate and most important connection in Bristol. This was the chief city authority, or Portreeve, of Bristol, Robert Fitzharding, who was also a close friend of the Norman King Henry II. Fitzharding, although it cannot be proven, may also have been a family connection. His wife had the very distinctive MacMurrough name of 'Aoife'. Before our story begins, Dermot had visited Fitzharding for a long conference (August 1166) in the abbey which Fitzharding had himself founded, the Augustinian Abbey, now Bristol Cathedral, commenced in 1142. It is probable that the actual place of their conference was the Chapter House. It is certainly one of the buildings Dermot and his men would have seen. It was Fitzharding who briefed Dermot on Strongbow and, for that matter, on Henry II.

# Ireland

**Baltinglass, County Wicklow:** One of Dermot Mac-Murrough's most beautiful foundations, both architecturally and for its setting, is Baltinglass Abbey, called 'Vallis Salutis'. He founded it for the great order of reformers, the Cistercians, in 1148. It enjoyed a colourful and turbulent history for four hundred years afterwards.

**Bannow Bay:** Here the first landing of Norman-led mercenaries arrived in 1169. They landed on the beaches just below the ruined church and sand-buried streets of the old port of Bannow.

**Dublin City:** Dublin City is particularly obliging in its sites of Dermot MacMurrough contact, for the explorer becomes involved in a torrent of history. Dermot Mac-Murrough's first foundation there was for an Abbey of Augustinian Nuns in 1146. It was named St. Mary de Hogges and is identified today as St. Andrew's Church in Suffolk Street. Not far away is the site of one of his most lasting and famous memorials; Dublin University or Trinity College, Dublin, was founded by Dermot MacMurrough in 1166 (just before his dramatic political collapse which sent him seeking mercenaries) as a Priory for Augustinian Canons dedicated to All Saints ('All Hallows'). One of the witnesses of his foundation charter was his wife's brother, Laurence O'Toole, the new Gaelic Archbishop of Norse Dublin, previously Abbot of Glendalough; he was later cannonised saint. The Priory was dissolved by Henry VIII in 1538, and in 1591 his daughter, Elizabeth I, had the College of the Most Holy Trinity erected in its place. The Augustinian Abbey's medieval and subsequent records are preserved, and are still to be seen and studied in Trinity's Library.

The sites of Viking Dublin in the Dublin Castle, Christ Church, St. Patrick's Cathedral and Wood Quay sector of the city are exceptionally well documented, and a visit to the Viking Dublin exhibits of the National Museum is to be recommended with enthusiasm. The remains of Strongbow, and probably his son and his second wife, Aoife, lie in Christ Church Cathedral.

**Dun Donnell or Baginbun** (as it was afterwards named): On the Hook peninsula below Fethard-on-Sea, this is one of the most dramatic sites associated with the Norman landings. The formidable twelfth century earthen defences are still to be seen, as well as the cliffs and little peninsula over which the wretched Viking prisoners, their legs broken by Raymond le Gros' men, were thrown. Its vital strategic importance was still recognized early in the last century, when an anti-Napoleonic construction called a Martello tower, now a private residence, was built.

**Ferns, County Wexford:** This is now a modest country village, albeit a prosperous one, in the middle of rich soils. Its records stretch back over fifteen centuries, and it has plenty of remains directly connected with Dermot. It was here, presumably in the earlier stone castle of Ferns upon which the present castle was expanded, or in the vicinity, that Dermot was born in 1110. Later it was the capital from which he ruled and where he died; his tomb, marked by the granite stump of a desecrated Celtic cross, is at the eastern side of Ferns Cathedral. The Abbey he founded himself at Ferns,

*Reginald's Tower*

close by the Cathedral, is identified by a typical Irish monastic round tower but with a square base. St. Peter's Church, across the little valley from the Cathedral, was thriving in his lifetime.

The destruction suffered by Ferns was due to its enormous political and religious significance. Whoever physically possessed Ferns possessed power, and in the centuries of battle and feud the defeated, or about-to-be defeated, were determined to leave little in the victor's hands. Ferns was utterly devastated after Cromwell's campaign of 1649.

**Passage, County Waterford:** Strongbow and his experienced contingent rounded the Hook peninsula, where no doubt they were recognized by Raymond le Gros' look-outs at Dun Donnell (or Baginbun) as they approached land. The village near the bend on the coast of Waterford Harbour is known as Passage East, and it was here, in a prime location to launch an attack on Waterford, that Strongbow landed without incident on 23 August 1170.

117

It is possible to land there today, too, without incident.  A very convenient car ferry plies between the two charming villages of Passage, County Waterford, and Ballyhack, County Wexford.

**Waterford City:** Considerable parts of Viking Waterford and its walls can still be explored with the aid of the Bord Fáilte (Irish Tourist Board) Guide Book. Reginald's Tower, the last of three on the triangle points of Waterford's walls, still exists on the south end of the Quay. Probably the most formidable of all Viking defensive remains in Ireland, it was built in 1003. Its history is reflected in an impressive display within of artifacts and memorabilia from Waterford's past. It is open to the public.

**Wexford Town:** The Viking citadel is still a military base; the present military barracks now occupies the site. By a further coincidence the area known as the Deadery (graveyard), where fierce fighting took place in front of the strongly defended Viking walls in 1169, is now the Garda (Police) Barracks; they were built over the then still existing graveyard in the late 1930s. A row of houses, to which steps indicate a sharp rise of ground, was built on top of the rock outcrop (opposite the Garda Barracks) from which the Norman archers showered arrows on the Viking defenders.

The unfortified Gaelic or native Irish part of the town was based around the present Corn Market and Selskar Abbey.

## *Wales*

**Pembroke Castle:** This castle, apart from Strongbow's connection with it, teems with interest. It was one

118

*Striguil (Chepstow) Castle*

of the best known Welsh fortresses in Dermot's era, even before it, since it was built in 1090 AD. In view of the many mercenary exchanges between Wales and Leinster in Dermot's lifetime, and the religious pilgrimages from his kingdom to St. David's Shrine and Cathedral, this would have been a well known area. It is of unusual interest that the descendant of Dermot and inheritor of the title, 'The MacMurrough-Kavanagh', resides today in Pembroke.

**Striguil Castle:** Chepstow is the modern name for Striguil, or, in Welsh, *Cas Gwent.* The castle, to which Strongbow was reduced when he was forced to leave Pembroke on the accession of the man he had opposed, Henry II, was first built in the mid-eleventh century, sixty or more years before Strongbow, following the Norman conquest of England.

On Strongbow's death, Striguil reverted to Henry II, because Isabel, Strongbow and Aoife's surviving child, was made a ward of court. She lived at Striguil in some style, according to Alan Reid (*Castles of Wales*), protected by a royal constable, a chaplain and his clerk, a porter, three watchmen, two men-at-arms, ten archers, and a further fifteen men-at-arms for whom it was their base camp.

# The People in
# Dermot MacMurrough's Life

As usually happens after the departure of a dominant administrator, a period of incohesion followed Dermot's last illness and death. It confused many historians, especially as there was a profusion of Norman documentation compared with a scarcity of Irish documentation. That itself is significant. There were two cultures, two sets of rules, two legal codes, two moral laws, two separate traditions, the Brehon Code for the Irish, Feudal Law for the Normans, the one incomprehensible to the other; that is until the Normans were absorbed and intermarried.

The earliest confusion surrounded the right of the inheritance of ruling power.

**The MacMurrough Succession:** Strongbow took MacMurrough at his word, i.e. that he was entitled to the Kingship of Leinster by right of his wife, Aoife, daughter of Dermot. The Irish side, of course, had quite clear and contrary parameters. A king has to be *elected* from the family of *male royal blood only,* by a senate of hereditary officials. The Regnal list in the Book of Leinster records that the men who succeeded Dermot Mac-Murrough as King of Uí Chinsealaigh were his brother Murrough (who ruled while Dermot, technically deposed, was seeking mercenaries); Dermot's son, born out of wedlock, Donal MacMurrough Kavanagh; and then Murtagh MacMurrough, son of the Murrough previously mentioned.

Thus two lines were established — the Mac-Murroughs and the MacMurrough Kavanaghs. The chief ruling power in MacMurrough's kingdom was ultimately achieved in Irish law by Donal Mac-Murrough Kavanagh's line. The principal surviving castle of the MacMurrough Kavanaghs today, the residence of Dermot's descendant, Andrew MacMurrough Kavanagh, and family, is Borris, County Carlow (visits by arrangement). The descendant of the MacMurrough line, with the title 'The O'Morchoe', lives at Ardgarry, Gorey, County Wexford.

Whatever claims Strongbow made to his feudal peers and monarch, by the August after Dermot's death he had made peace with the new King of Uí Chinsealaigh, Murrough, and spent some days with him in Ferns Castle.

The leading Norman knights elected to remain in Ireland to carve out estates and power for themselves, acting as mercenaries the while for several Irish royal families, accepting feudal titles from their monarch in a confusing if determined 'free for all'. Overlapping titles and claims vied for legality and fought for acceptance in periodic outbursts until the final great leveller, Oliver Cromwell, devasted the old order for ever in 1649–1650.

**Strongbow and Aoife** had an enduring but short marriage. Their one daughter, Isabel, created a maze of family connections across Norman England to complement her own substantial connections at home. Isabel, Dermot's grand-daughter, married William de Mareschal, Norman Earl Marshal of England, Viceroy in Ireland (i.e. the Norman King's deputy), 'Senechal (Steward) of Leinster', which titles he retained in Ireland until 1194. Through Isabel, as the daughter of

121

Strongbow and grand-daughter of Dermot Mac-
Murrough, William le Mareschal inherited vast
territories in England as well as any property claimed by
Strongbow and Aoife in Leinster.

William and Isabel had five sons and five daughters.
Remarkable to relate, all five sons died without issue,
but the five daughters each married Norman noblemen
and had issue.

Another of Dermot's grand-daughters, the daughter
of Donal O'Brien, King of Thomond, married another
Norman leader, William de Burgh.

Strongbow was compelled after Dermot's death to
live out his life in battle in Ireland and mainland
Europe, where he won himself back into the scarce
esteem of his King, Henry II, and was restored to his
estates and title of Pembroke. He died of a foot ulcer in
Dublin in 1176 and is buried in Christ Church
Cathedral, Dublin. He had only survived his father-in-
law by five years.

**De la Roche:** De la Roche and his contingent were
Flemish. There were granted the land east across Wexford's inner harbour, where their first castle still exists.
Their stone guard tower at the Slaney's Ferry Carraig is
one of the prominent features, much photographed, at
the approaches to the Heritage Park. The direct Wexford descendants of De la Roche live today at nearby
Garrylough, Screen, on the same lands, but after centuries of strife, confiscation, eviction, return and rebel-
lion.

**Raymond le Gros** married Strongbow's sister, and
like his brother-in-law spent his remaining active years
in various campaigns in Ireland and abroad. He retired

peacefully to his holdings near Cork, where he died in 1186.

**Robert FitzStephen** seemed destined from birth for a sword or dungeon life. He was 'granted' lands in County Kerry and County Cork, provided he could win and hold them by force of arms. He was killed, along with a fellow Norman knight, Milo de Cogan, in 1182.

**Henry II,** King of the Normans, was thoroughly alarmed at the freebooter Norman adventures in Ireland, which he had expressly forbidden. His fear was galvanized by the death of Dermot MacMurrough. Fearing then that a rival Norman kingdom which would replace the Norsemen, or some other competing association might be set up, he decided to intervene personally to limit the power of his barons. He landed near Waterford late in 1171 with four thousand men, twice the number of Norman mercenaries then in Ireland. With the exception of Rory O'Connor and the Northern Ireland rulers the remaining Irish kings made the usual Irish submissions; in other words, submission only for as long as it suited. Under feudal law, of course, the submission was held to be permanent, full stop!

Henry gave the barons he suspected back-breaking tasks, and introduced a trusted cohort, Hugh de Lacy, to rule the captured Norse city of Dublin and the County of Meath. Henry also conferred with and ameliorated the Church authorities and the Papal Legate in Ireland. He spent Christmas 1171 in Dublin, and the Lenten season of 1172 in Wexford doing penance. He left Wexford for Wales on Easter Monday and never returned to Ireland again.

**Rory O'Connor,** King of Connaught, (High) King of

Ireland. Three years after Henry II left Ireland, in October 1975, Rory O'Connor, the last clearly acknowledged or accepted King of All Ireland, signed the Treaty of Windsor. Under this, he recognized Henry as lord and Henry recognized him as (High) King of Gaelic Ireland. In the Irish concept of law that would be accepted as an arrangement of mutual convenience without permanence.

By contrast with MacMurrough's family, Rory O'Connor's life and family were torn by internal strife and bloodshed. He died in 1198, in retirement.

**Ros,** Rory's daughter, may have been the girl proposed by him to wed the ill-fated Conor MacMurrough. She eventually married the most dominant of the Norman knights favoured by Henry II, Hugh de Lacy.

**Tiernan O'Rourke,** King of Bréifne. The hatred between Dermot MacMurrough and Tiernan O'Rourke had been of lifelong duration for both men, O'Rourke being the probably unwitting instigator. One year after Dermot's death O'Rourke embarked on his final campaign, once more against long-suffering Meath. After several raids and the capture of numerous cattle it was recorded that 'the dog of war burned the Round Tower of Tullyard with its full of human beings'. He was finally captured by a contingent of Normans, aided, treacherously if appropriately, by one of his own clan, Donnell O'Rourke. He was beheaded and both head and body were borne back to Dublin. The head was put on display, 'raised over the gate of the fortress'. His body was hung feet upwards nearby; 'a sore miserable sight for the Gael', according to the entry in the *Annals of Ulster*.

**Maurice O'Regan,** Dermot MacMurrough's 'Secretary of State', his persistant and life-long loyal deputy, is suspected to be the author or at least to have supplied the information for one of the source works of Dermot's life, *The Song of Dermot and the Earl.*

# A Select Bibliography

Apart from the Irish Annals including the *Book of Leinster; The Song of Dermot and the Earl* (trans. by G. H. Orpen, Oxford) and Cambrensis' *Expugnatio Hibernica* (RIA 1978), the following short list of recently published or republished works helps to give succinct background information to the period and the remarkable career of Dermot MacMurrough, King of Leinster and the Foreigners, King of Uí Chinnsealaigh:

*Anglo Norman Ireland,* Michael Dolley, Gill History No. 3. Dublin 1972.

*Castles of Wales, The,* Alan Reid, Letts Guides.

*Dermot, King of Leinster and the Foreigners,* Nicholas Furlong, Anvil Books 1973.

*History of the Town and County of Wexford,* Vols 5 and 6, P. H. Hore, London 1911.

*Ireland before the Normans,* Donncha O Corrain, Gill History of Ireland, No 2. Dublin 1972.

*Irish Kings and High Kings,* Prof. Francis J. Byrne, London 1973.

*Norman Invasion of Ireland, The,* Richard Roche, Anvil Books 1970.

*Studia Hibernica, No 11. Irish Regnal Succession: A reappraisal.* Donncha O Corrain, Dublin 1971.

## *Nicholas Furlong*

Nicholas Furlong, Wexford writer and farmer, was born in 1929. Educated at CBS, Wexford, St. Peter's College, Wexford, and the Salesian Agricultural College, Warrenstown, County Meath, he has an Honours Diploma in Social and Economic Studies from UCD.

He had contributed to many journals, newspapers and television programmes, and published several historic papers, including five tour guides and *Dermot King of Leinster and the Foreigners* (Anvil 1972), the first and still the only biography of this controversial figure in Irish history.

His book of photographs of the Wexford region, *Wexford in the Rare Oul Times* (1850–1914), which he coauthored with John Hayes, was a bestseller at Christmas 1985.

Three of his dramatic works have been produced by

Tomas MacAnna: *Insurrection '98* in 1965 in Dun Mhuire in Wexford; *The Lunatic Fringe* the following year, which resulted in nation-wide controversy; *Purple and Gold*, a stage production celebrating the centenary of the GAA, in 1984.

In 1977 he was elected a Fellow of the Royal Society of Antiquaries of Ireland, and became a Vice-President in 1979. He is a council member of the Wexford Opera Festival.

*A Foster Son for a King* is his first book for children.

# Hawthorn

is a new imprint for The Children's Press, and will appear on historical fiction. *A Foster Son for a King* is the first in the series. The second is *Murtagh and the Vikings*, by Roger Chatterton Newman.

On a wild dark night in 795, the first Viking raiders strike on Rathlin Island. Young Murtagh is captured and brought to Norway in a longboat. Befriended by the Viking chieftain, Erik Redbeard, he attends a great banquet, takes part in a reindeer hunt and becomes involved in a clan feud. But all the time he plots to escape, taking the Christian slaves with him. Will he succeed...?

Story and illustrations bring the Viking age brilliantly to life.

# Acorn

Adventure fiction for 9 to 12 year olds, in Irish settings.

## Also by The Children's Press